SLAVERY 101

❧ THE LOCHLAINN SEABROOK COLLECTION ❧

Five-Star Books & Gifts With Five-Star Service!

SeaRavenPress.com

SLAVERY 101

Amazing Facts You Never Knew
About America's "Peculiar Institution"

A highly condensed version of the author's massive scholarly work
Everything You Were Taught About American Slavery Is Wrong, Ask a Southerner!

LOCHLAINN SEABROOK

JEFFERSON DAVIS HISTORICAL GOLD MEDAL WINNER

ILLUSTRATED

SEA RAVEN PRESS, NASHVILLE, TENNESSEE, USA

SLAVERY 101

Published by
Sea Raven Press, Cassidy Ravensdale, President
PO Box 1484, Spring Hill, Tennessee 37174-1484 USA
SeaRavenPress.com • searavenpress@gmail.com

1st paperback edition, 1st printing: March 2015
1st paperback edition, 2nd printing: August 2015
1st hardcover edition, 1st printing (978-1-943737-04-8): August 2015

ISBN: 978-0-9913779-5-4 (paperback)
Library of Congress Control Number: 2015931234

Slavery 101: Amazing Facts You Never Knew About America's "Peculiar Institution," by
Lochlainn Seabrook. Includes an index, endnotes, and bibliographical references.

Front and back cover design and art, book design, layout, and interior art by Lochlainn Seabrook
Typography: Sea Raven Press Book Design
All images, graphic design, graphic art, and illustrations copyright © Lochlainn Seabrook
Cover image: "Typical Southern Tobacco Plantation 1859," courtesy U.S. Library of Congress
Cover image copyright © Lochlainn Seabrook
Portions of this book have been adapted from the author's other works

The views on the American "Civil War" documented in this book *are* those of the publisher.

The paper used in this book is acid-free and lignin-free. It has been certified by the Sustainable Forestry
Initiative and the Forest Stewardship Council and meets all ANSI standards for archival quality paper.

PRINTED & MANUFACTURED IN OCCUPIED TENNESSEE, FORMER CONFEDERATE STATES OF AMERICA

DEDICATION

TO MY ANGLO-SAXON, CELTIC, & ROMAN
SLAVE OWNING & SLAVE ANCESTORS

EPIGRAPH

"The people of the North and East are, or affect to be, totally ignorant of the actual state and character of our Negro Population; they represent the condition of their bondage as a perpetual revolution of labor and severity, rendered still more deplorable by an utter destitution of all the comforts of life. Our Negroes, according to these candid and accurate observers, are in every respect illy provided, badly fed and badly clothed; worked beyond their physical capacity while in health; neglected while in sickness; going always to their labor with the most dogged reluctance, confined to it by the severity of the cart-whip, and denied, in fine, all the ordinary enjoyments of existence. Now, the very reverse of this is the truth; and it is within the province of those who are continually defaming us, to ascertain it; yet, notwithstanding that the most abundant testimony is at hand to satisfy the most curious inquirer upon the subject, and every candid and enlightened observer finds himself at every step furnished with the most ample refutation of these charges, the calumny has nevertheless been industriously propagated and upheld with a malignity of design, and an utter contempt of truth, at war with every thing like fair argument, or the most ordinary regard for our feelings."

EDWIN CLIFFORD HOLLAND, 1822
SOUTH CAROLINA HISTORIAN

Southern "slaves."

CONTENTS

NOTES TO THE READER

☛ In any study of America's antebellum, bellum, and postbellum periods, it is vitally important to understand that in 1860 the two major political parties—the Democrats and the newly formed Republicans—were the opposite of what they are today. In other words, the Democrats of the mid 19th Century were Conservatives, akin to the Republican Party of today, while the Republicans of the mid 19th Century were Liberals, akin to the Democratic Party of today.

Thus the Confederacy's Democratic president, Jefferson Davis, was a Conservative (with libertarian leanings); the Union's Republican president, Abraham Lincoln, was a Liberal (with socialistic leanings). This is why, in the mid 1800s, the conservative wing of the Democratic Party was known as "the States' Rights Party."[1]

The author's cousin, Confederate Vice President and Democrat Alexander H. Stephens: a Southern Conservative.

Hence, the Democrats of the Civil War period referred to themselves as "conservatives," "confederates," "anti-centralists," or "constitutionalists" (the latter because they favored strict adherence to the original Constitution—which tacitly guaranteed states' rights—as created by the Founding Fathers), while the Republicans called themselves "liberals," "nationalists," "centralists," or "consolidationists" (the latter three because they wanted to nationalize the central government and consolidate political power in Washington, D.C.).[2]

Since this idea is new to most of my readers, let us further demystify it by viewing it from the perspective of the American Revolutionary War. If Davis and his conservative Southern constituents (the Democrats of 1861) had been alive in 1775, they would have sided with George Washington and the American colonists, who sought to secede from the tyrannical government of Great Britain; if Lincoln and his Liberal Northern constituents (the Republicans of 1861) had been alive at that time, they would have sided with King George III and the English monarchy, who sought to maintain the American colonies as possessions of the British Empire. It is due to this very comparison that Southerners often refer to the "Civil War" as the Second American Revolutionary War.

☛ As I heartily dislike the phrase "Civil War," its use throughout this book (as well as in my other works) is worthy of an explanation.

Today America's entire literary system refers to the conflict of 1861 using the Northern term the "Civil War," whether we in the South like it or not. Thus, as all book searches by readers, libraries, and retail outlets are now performed online, and as all bookstores categorize works from this period under the heading "Civil War," book publishers and authors who deal with this particular topic have little choice but to use this term themselves. If I were to refuse to use it, as some of my Southern colleagues have suggested, few people would ever find or read my books.

Add to this the fact that scarcely any non-Southerners have ever heard of the names we in the South use for the conflict, such as the "War for Southern Independence"—or my personal preference, "Lincoln's War." It only makes sense then to use the term "Civil War" in most commercial situations.

We should also bear in mind that while today educated persons, particularly educated Southerners, all share an abhorrence for the phrase "Civil War," it was not always so. Confederates who lived through and even fought in the conflict regularly used the term throughout the 1860s, and even long after. Among them were Confederate generals such as Nathan Bedford Forrest, Richard Taylor, and Joseph E. Johnston, not to mention the Confederacy's vice president, Alexander H. Stephens. Even the Confederacy's highest leader, President Jefferson Davis, used the term "Civil War,"[3] and in one case at least, as late as 1881—the year he wrote his brilliant exposition, *The Rise and Fall of the Confederate Government*.[4]

☛ Neither slavery or Lincoln's War on the American people and the Constitution can ever be fully understood without a thorough knowledge of the South's perspective. As *Slavery 101* is only meant to be a brief introductory guide to these topics, one cannot hope to learn the whole truth about them here. For those who are interested in a more in-depth study, please see my other more scholarly books, listed on page 2; in particular, my title, *Everything You Were Taught About American Slavery is Wrong, Ask a Southerner!*

THE NORTH IS STILL LYING ABOUT LINCOLN'S WAR

INTRODUCTION

T hose with an interest in learning the facts about American slavery will never get them from our mainstream history books, most of whose politically correct and intolerant authors are virulently anti-South; graduates of socialistic universities who write according to the biased agenda of Northern liberalism. But why what I call "The Great Yankee Coverup"?[5] For the same reason you are not supposed to know the truth about the so-called "Civil War."

Abraham Lincoln was a big government Liberal who, like all progressives, not only disliked the Constitution, but desired total dictatorial control over the

American people, economy, and military. When the Southern states seceded he saw this control slipping away, along with the lucrative "revenue" the U.S. government once derived from the Yankee slave trade (which sold its human products southward) and the wealth of resources provided by Dixie and her 12 million people (all races). Lincoln's response was to trick the South into firing the first shot at the Battle of Fort Sumter, drawing the Confederacy into a four year long conflict that left little but desolation, grief, destruction, and countless thousands dead in its wake.

To protect the Liberal establishment's reputation and, more importantly, justify Lincoln's illegal, irrational, and immoral assault on the Constitution and the American people, a convincing "motivation" had to be fabricated, and that "motivation" was Southern slavery. It is in this fashion that the Left Wing, pro-North, and pro-Lincoln movements have been suppressing the truth about both the War and American slavery for the past 150 years.

As a Southern historian I believe it is time that the truth be told in an honest and historically accurate way, and *Slavery 101: Amazing Facts You Never Knew About America's "Peculiar Institution"*—a highly condensed version of my much larger work, *Everything You Were Taught About American Slavery is Wrong, Ask a Southerner!*—intends to do just that. May this little book inspire a new appreciation for both the Truth and the South for generations to come.

Lochlainn Seabrook
Nashville, Tennessee, USA
March 2015

FACT 1

SLAVERY IS NOT A "PECULIAR INSTITUTION"
IT IS A UNIVERSAL INSTITUTION

Since American black slavery was not a domestic phenomenon, but rather the end product of thousands of years of worldwide slavery that got its start in Africa, we must begin our study from an international perspective.

The uninformed have long referred to American slavery, and more specifically Southern slavery, as the "peculiar institution." Actually, there was nothing "peculiar" about it, and neither was it Southern, for it was once a common worldwide practice.

Indeed, slavery has been embraced by every known civilization, people, race, society, culture, and religion around the globe, from earliest recorded history right into present-day America. Some of the more notable slaving peoples have been the Egyptians, Assyrians, Babylonians, Sumerians, Akkadians, Mesopotamians, Phoenicians, Mycenaeans, Arameans, East Indians, Chaldeans, Hittites, Scythians, Persians, Arabians, Hebrews, Europeans, and Native-Americans, all who have a long history of enslaving their own citizens and their neighbors.

Slavery has existed in every society, on every continent, among every people, since prehistoric times. To call it anything but a universal institution is a flagrant deception and a gross distortion of reality.

An institution that has been found among nearly every people and on every continent since prehistoric times can hardly be considered "peculiar." In fact, as this very book shows, it would be more appropriately and accurately called the universal, standard, ordinary, or everyday institution.[6]

FACT 2

HUMAN CIVILIZATION COULD NOT HAVE ARISEN WITHOUT SLAVERY

S lavery was once so integral to the economies of early human cultures that civilization itself would not exist without it. Slavery formed the very underpinnings, for example, of such ancient lands as Rome and Greece, out of which all of Western society evolved.

In Greece—where slavery (chiefly white slavery) was considered a prerequisite for the building and maintenance of Greek society—there was literally no known time at which she did not practice the institution. The result was that there were no Greek states in which slaves did not outnumber the free inhabitants.

One estimate puts the ancient free Greek population at 5 million (29 percent) and the slave population at 12 million (71 percent). Translated into modern terms, if these numbers were applied to 21st-Century America, we would today have nearly 700 million white slaves catering to the needs of our free population of just over 300 million.[7]

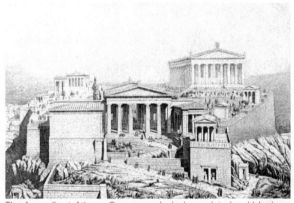

The Acropolis at Athens, Greece, overlooked a society in which slaves greatly outnumbered freemen, typical in the ancient world.

FACT 3

WE ALL DESCEND FROM
SLAVES & SLAVE OWNERS

No one knows who actually invented slavery of course, for it was a worldwide phenomenon that arose simultaneously around the globe. But we do know that it dates from prehistory, was once universally accepted on every part of the planet, and that at one time it was found on every continent, in every single nation, and among every people, race, religion, and ethnic group. As one historian puts it, "so far as we can trace back the history of the human race, we discover the existence of slavery."

Slavery was, in fact, the economic system upon which *all* ancient civilizations were built, for "slavery is the precursor to civilization." As such it must certainly be counted as one of humanity's oldest social institutions and an essential feature of both society and economics. It is, as the *Encyclopedia Britannica* says, a universal, useful, indispensable, and inevitable accompaniment of human culture, one that eventually became so taken for granted that it was seen as a "divinely ordained institution" in every country.

In 1837, America's seventh vice president, South Carolinian John C. Calhoun, rightly noted that

> there has never yet existed a wealthy and civilized society in which one portion of the community did not, in fact, live on the labor of the other.

This means that slavery is a natural byproduct of human society, placing it alongside our other oldest human social institutions: hunting and gathering, religion, marriage, warfare, puberty rites, funerary rites, and prostitution.[8] Indeed, anthropologists consider slavery not an indication of barbarity, but an early sign of civilization: its emergence meant that humans had begun to enslave rather than kill one another.

From its appearance in the prehistoric mists of time, slavery went on to be employed by the Mesopotamians (ancient Iraqis), Indians, Chinese, ancient Egyptians, Hebrews, Greeks, and Romans. In the pre-Columbian Americas slavery became an integral part of such Native-American peoples as the Maya and Inca, who depended on large scale slave labor in warfare and farming.

The reality is that slavery is a worldwide, omnipresent phenomenon, one that stubbornly persists into modern times, and which dates far back into the fog of the Neolithic Period on all continents, and among all races, ethnic groups, religions, societies, and peoples. All of us then, no matter what our race, color, or nationality, have ancestors who enslaved others and who were themselves enslaved. *We are all descendants of slaves and slave owners.*[9]

Native-Americans have been enslaving their own kind, and later whites and blacks, since time immemorial. These Aztecs are sacrificing one of their many slaves.

FACT 4

AFRICA HAS ALWAYS BEEN THE MOST SLAVE DEPENDENT REGION IN THE WORLD

No region on earth has been more dependent on slavery over a longer period of time, practiced slavery more aggressively and widely on its own populace, or allowed slavery to become more entrenched, than Africa. Africa has been so intimately involved with slavery over such an immense duration—with slave majorities thought to be as high as 90 percent of the population in some regions—that its name is today synonymous with the institution. "The great womb of slavery," Yankee abolitionist Charles Sumner correctly called it.

Slavery was so intrinsic to the early African way of life that at one time slaves, known by their own people as "black ivory," could be found in nearly every African society, where—as in every other country where slavery is found—the minority population dominated and enslaved the majority population. These were not merely "insignificant traces of slavery," as African apologists maintain, but rather true African slave societies, built on and around the bondage of their own people, employing some of the most brutal and sadistic forms of slavery ever recorded.

Slavery's pivotal role in African society certainly explains why not a single organized slave revolt, or even an abolition movement for that matter, ever arose among the African populace during the entire pre-colonial period, and it is why slavery was finally only outlawed by the efforts of non-Africans (mainly Europeans).

It also explains why there has long been a belief among the native population that due to domestic African slavery, "the whole land has been laid under a curse which will never be removed."[10]

FACT 5

AFRICAN SLAVERY BEGAN
IN AFRICA, NOT AMERICA

Africans were practicing slavery on themselves for thousands of years before the arrival of Europeans. In point of fact, "African slavery was coeval with the existence of the African race . . . . [and thus] has existed in Africa since its first [negro] settlement," predating even the founding of ancient Egypt over 5,000 years ago.

It cannot be stressed enough that, it being a "characteristic part of African tradition" and a truly "universal" aspect of African society, *African slavery was of African origin.* Thus indigenous African slavery is nearly as old as Africa itself. Indeed, not only were slaves an integral part of the commerce of prehistoric and ancient Africa, but just as in early Sudan, as only one example, slave ownership was an accepted sign of wealth, and so was considered no different than owning precious metals or gems. Even the practice of exporting African slaves out of the country can be definitively dated back to at least the 5th Century B.C. It can be truly said then that *early Africa literally revolved around the enslavement of its own people by its own rulers upon its own soil.*

The native victims of the pre-conquest African slave trade were captured inland or in East Africa by their African brethren, then exported to Persia, Arabia, India, and China. This means that the first European slavers to venture to Africa (Portuguese ship captain Antonio Gonzales arrived in 1434 and purchased several native African boys who he sold in Spain, while Portugal's trade in slaves with the continent began in 1441) only interrupted the booming, "well-developed" slave trade inaugurated by West Africans and various coastal tribes—one that had already been going on there for untold centuries with peoples like the Arabs. It was only much later that Europeans helped stimulate the existing domestic business.[11]

FACT 6

AFRICA ENGAGED IN THE TRANSATLANTIC SLAVE TRADE FOR ITS ENTIRE 424 YEARS

Pre-European Africa had been practicing slavery, servitude, vassalage, and serfdom on its own people for thousands of years (in forms far more brutal than anything found in the American South), dating back to before the continent's Iron Age, to the very dawn of African history itself. In fact, Africa is the *only* region that engaged *continually* in the West African-European-American slave trade for its full 424 years, from start to finish.

It was just such facts that made the institution so understandable to many American black civil rights leaders. One of these was African-American educator, intellectual, and author William E. B. Du Bois, who wrote that he could forgive slavery for it "is a world-old habit."[12]

All early African peoples once enslaved each other. Slaves were procured mainly through vicious intertribal raids and constant warfare, as this old illustration shows. Note the baby being thrown in the air and speared, and the beheading and dismemberment of the conquered. Those who survived these barbaric attacks were enslaved for life, usually under the ownership of a neighboring African king.

FACT 7

AFRICA IS RESPONSIBLE FOR ENSLAVING & SELLING HER OWN PEOPLE

W hat Yankee historians, New South professors, and the Liberal media will not tell you is that Africans were never actually hunted down and captured directly by the white crews of foreign slave ships. They were captives who had already been taken during yearly intertribal raids and then enslaved by enterprising African kings, kinglets, chiefs, and subchiefs, who quite eagerly traded them to non-African slavers for rum, guns, gunpowder, textiles, beads, iron, and cloth.

Sometimes these intra-African militaristic style raids and battles were carried on by slave armies led by slave officers. Though the attrition rate was extremely high (over the millennia millions upon millions of Africans died during these marauding attacks), greedy African kings would often purposefully start such wars, known as "slave hunts," in order to obtain slaves, a practice that eventually became "endemic" across large swaths of the continent.

In other words, it was African chiefs who first enslaved other Africans, and it was African slave merchants—slave drivers known as *Slattees*—who then forcibly marched them to the coast in chains and sold them to Arabs, Europeans, and eventually Yankees. This means that when it came to African slaves, *all* of the slave hunting, slave capturing, slave abusing, slave torturing, slave marching, slave marketing, slave dealing, and slave selling went on *inside* Africa, perpetuated by Africans on other Africans on African land.

This is why before 1820 no free blacks ever came to the U.S. from Africa. All were imported as slaves—that is, they were already in bondage in their native country.

To put it another way, during the transatlantic slave trade, every one of the Africans brought to America on Yankee slave ships had already been enslaved in their home country by fellow Africans, after which they were marched to the Slave Coast (a 240-mile maritime strip roughly extending between the Volta River and the Akinga River), temporarily held in stockades (prisons), then sold to white slavers by local African governments.

In short, whites only "bought slaves after they had been captured," and thus played no role in the actual enslaving process that took place in the interior, and had no idea what went on beyond the coastal areas. As one Yankee slave ship owner put it in the late 1700s:

> It is true, I have brought these slaves from Africa; but I have only transported them from one master to another.

Yes, *African slavery was purely an African-on-African business.*

And here is proof: until the first part of the 19th Century, no white man had ever set foot in the interior of tropical Africa. Even the Europeans who first came to Africa's shores in the 1400s had no knowledge of anything "south of the desert." These were the African hinterlands, after all: utterly unnavigable and therefore unexplorable, due in great part to the ferocity of the native animals, and to the fact that it swarmed with cannibalistic tribes who practiced human sacrifice and other primitive customs.

At one time even radical abolitionists admitted as much. In 1835 Reverend George Bourne—the Briton who inspired fanatical New England abolitionist William Lloyd Garrison—noted that "no ancient and accessible part of the inhabited globe is so completely unknown as the interior of Africa." Thus whites could not have had any knowledge of what went on in the central regions of the continent during most of the Atlantic slave trade.

Truly, without Africa's encouragement, commitment, participation, and collusion there would have been no black slavery in America. It is obvious then that Africa herself must be held accountable for taking part in the enslavement and forced deportation of some 10 to 50 million of her own people during the four hundred years between the 15th and the 19th Centuries.[13]

FACT 8

WHITE SLAVERY WAS ONCE
A WORLDWIDE PHENOMENA

Our leftist schools focus only on black slavery, completely ignoring the reality of white slavery—and for good reason: America's liberalistic teachers do not want the truth to be known, for it would expose and demolish their false teachings about racism and capitalism. Here we will correct this imbalance.

Not only did American slavery exist among native peoples—for example, the Aztecs, Incas, and Mayans—long before the arrival of Christopher Columbus (the man responsible for starting the European-American slave trade), but Western slavery itself began as a purely white man's occupation, one that had nothing to do with Indians, Africans, or any other people of color, or even racism.

Indeed, historically speaking, *both the earliest known slave traders and the earliest known slaves were Caucasians*: the Babylonians, Assyrians, Sumerians, Akkadians, Mesopotamians, Phoenicians, Egyptians, Mycenaeans, Arameans, East Indians, Chaldeans, Hittites, Scythians, Persians, Arabians, and Hebrews—at some point in their history—all either enslaved other whites or were themselves enslaved by other whites. In India, for example, historic records show that Caucasian slavery was being practiced by 1750 B.C., nearly 4,000 years ago, though doubtlessly it arose there thousands of years earlier. Some maintain that white thralldom may have even once been an integral part of Hinduism, one of the world's oldest religions.

The Vikings, Celts, Greeks, Italians, British, French, and, in fact, all European peoples, once enslaved other whites, a practice that has endured into the present day: in the 1940s Adolf Hitler enslaved nearly 8 million Caucasians, while in the 1930s Joseph Stalin enslaved as many as 18 million whites.[14]

FACT 9

AFRICA ONCE POSSESSED
1.5 MILLION WHITE SLAVES

At one time there were so many white slaves in Africa that a series of wars, known as the Barbary Wars, were fought and an abolition society, known as the "Knights Liberators of the White Slaves in Africa," was formed to rescue and emancipate them.

The primary period of the enslavement of whites by African peoples lasted some 300 years, roughly from the 16th Century to the 19th Century. It has been conservatively estimated that between the years 1500 and 1800, 1 million to 1.5 million whites—from both Europe and America—were enslaved by the Barbary States, with an average of 5,000 white slaves entering the region each year. At about 14 new whites being imported a day, it was a commonplace occurrence. The city of Algiers, the capital of the African nation of Algeria, alone possessed some 25,000 to 50,000 European bondsmen and women. Over the centuries countless tens of thousands of additional whites were killed during the process of enslavement.

Africa once enslaved over a million whites.

The Barbary Wars were comprised of several full scale U.S. military campaigns, launched in an effort to put a stop to the merciless enslavement of white Christians in Africa: the Tripolitan War (or First Barbary War, 1801-1805) under President Thomas Jefferson, and the Algerian War (or Second Barbary War, 1815) under President James Madison. Shortly thereafter, in 1816, the British, led by Lord Exmouth (Edward Pellew), conducted their own assault on African white slavery in the famed conflict known as the "Battle of Algiers."[15]

FACT 10

AFRICAN SLAVE OWNERS TREATED THEIR WHITE & BLACK SLAVES FAR WORSE THAN ANYTHING KNOWN IN AMERICA

Surviving records reveal that Africa's black slave owners treated both their black and white slaves with absolute savagery, daily subjecting them to appalling forms of abuse and even torture that included whipping, branding, starvation, exposure, and beheading. One example of how they treated their personal African slaves will suffice:

> On the death of a king, or a distinguished [African] chief, hundreds of their courtiers, wives, and slaves are put to death, in order that they may have the benefit of their attendance in the future world. It often happens, that where the sword of the rude warrior is once drawn in such cases, it is not again readily sheathed; whole towns may be depopulated before the thirst for blood is satiated.

Thus in 1800 the funeral of Ashanti King Quamina was accompanied by the ritual murder of 200 African slaves. On another occasion the Ashanti people slaughtered some 2,600 African slaves at a single public sacrifice. In 1873, when the British seized Kumasi, a city in southern central Ghana, they discovered a huge brass bowl five feet in diameter. In it the Ashanti had collected the blood of countless thousands of sacrificed African slaves and used it to wash the footstools of deceased African kings.

Once, when the mother of a certain Ashanti king died, 3,000 African slaves were sacrificed at her tomb, and for two months afterward 200 additional slaves were put to death every week "in her honor." Did anything in the American South ever compare to such horrific savagery?[16]

FACT 11

THE TRANSATLANTIC SLAVE TRADE PROVIDED AT LEAST ONE BENEFIT TO AFRICA

Though we are quite familiar with the many real horrors of the transatlantic slave trade, few have acknowledged that it also benefitted Africa in at least one way: by increasing the monetary value of African slaves, it greatly reduced instances of their abuse, torture, murder, and sacrifice by fellow Africans.[17]

The transatlantic slave trade could not have arisen without the enthusiasm and efforts of Africa. The trade, though mainly harmful to African society, actually benefitted African slaves themselves.

FACT 12

WHITE AMERICAN SLAVERY LAID THE GROUNDWORK FOR BLACK AMERICAN SLAVERY

The vast majority of white immigrants who came to America's original 13 English colonies—at least two-thirds—came as white servants. Made up primarily of English, Germans, Irish, and Scots, some 400,000 whites formed the first non-American servant population in the region's history, working as unskilled laborers on the budding nation's large new plantations.

White indentured servitude, being much preferred over African slavery (Africans were considered "alien" by early white colonialists), *was the institution that paved the way for black slavery in America*; or as the late 19th-Century New England historian Jeffrey R. Brackett put it, white slavery made "a smoother pathway for the growth of [black] slavery." In 1698, as just one example, not only were there more white servants in Virginia than there were Africans, but white indentured servants were being imported in far greater numbers than blacks at the time.[18]

A white mother and daughter for sale on the auction block. In America black slavery was only possible because of the nationwide institution of white slavery that preceded it.

FACT 13

IN EARLY AMERICA A WHITE SLAVE WAS WORTH LESS THAN HALF THAT OF A BLACK SLAVE.

illions of 17th- and 18th-Century Europeans came to America as servants, or in some cases as slaves. President Martin Van Buren's third great-grandfather, for example, Cornelius Maesen Van Buren, emigrated from the Netherlands to New York as an indentured servant. Henry Wilson, President Ulysses S. Grant's second vice president and a cofounder of the Free-Soil Party, worked as an indentured slave for eleven years, from age ten to 21. Even one of Abraham Lincoln's ancestors, an early relation who was part of the Massachusetts Bay Colony, came to America as an indentured servant.

Thirteen of the 30 members of Virginia's House of Burgesses came across the Atlantic as indentured servants, as did Adam Thoroughgood, the founder of the city of Norfolk, Virginia. It was Virginia that passed the nation's first white servitude bill on July 30, 1619, legalizing the institution of white slavery within its borders. Noted Victorian historian George Bancroft of Massachusetts writes:

> Conditional servitude, under indentures or covenants, had from the first existed in Virginia. Once at least [King] James [I] sent over convicts, and once at least the city of London a hundred homeless children from its streets. The servant stood to his master in the relation of a debtor, bound to discharge by his labor the costs of emigration. White servants came to be a usual article of merchandise. They were sold in England to be transported, and in Virginia were to be purchased on shipboard. Not the Scots only, who were taken in the field of Dunbar, were sold into servitude in New England, but the royalist prisoners of the battle of Worcester. The leaders in the insurrection of Penruddoc, in spite of the remonstrance of [Sir Arthur] Haselrig and Henry Vane, were

shipped to America. At the corresponding period, in Ireland, the exportation of Irish Catholics was frequent. In 1672, the average price in the colonies, where five years of service were due, was about ten pounds, while a negro was worth twenty or twenty-five pounds.[19]

Two out of three early white immigrants entered North America as a servant or slave.

FACT 14

THE AMERICAN BLACK SLAVE TRADE BEGAN IN THE NORTH

C ontrary to what we have been taught, America's black slave trade was not born in the South. It was a product of the North. This is why the only slave ships to ever sail from the U.S. left from Northern ports, this is why all were commanded by Northern captains and funded by Northern businessmen, and it is why all of them operated under the auspices of the U.S. flag.

The South did not engage in the slave trade, which is why slave ports, like this one in New England, did not exist in Dixie.

The South, on the other hand, did not own slave ships and never traded in foreign slaves. Her slavery was strictly domestic. This is one of the reasons she banned the foreign slave trade in the Confederacy's new Constitution, penned by the Confederate Founding Fathers in 1861. Thus, while no slave ship ever flew under the Confederate Flag, it is this very flag that is today universally viewed as a "symbol of slavery"!

Early Northern politicians were well aware that they could not fool the public about the origins of slavery simply by deflecting the entire issue onto the South. One of these was U.S. Representative Jonathan Ogden Mosely of Connecticut. When, in the late 1700s, the idea of executing slave ship owners by hanging came up before a congressional committee on abolition, the Yankee politician remarked:

We have been repeatedly told, and told with an air of triumph, by gentlemen from the South, that *their citizens have no concern in this infamous traffic; that people from the North are the importers of negroes, and thereby the seducers of Southern citizens to buy them.* We have a right to presume, then, that the citizens of the South will entertain no particular partiality for these wicked traffickers, but will be ready to subject them to the most exemplary punishment. So far as the people of Connecticut are concerned, I am sure that, should any citizen of the North be convicted under this law, so far from thinking it cruel in their Southern brethren to hang them, such a punishment of such culprits would be acknowledged with gratitude as a favor.[20]

Now we can better understand the words of U.S. Senator Jefferson Davis, soon to become the Southern Confederacy's first and—so far—only president, who, in 1848, rightly chastised his Northern brethren on the Senate floor for their abolitionist hypocrisy:

You were the men who imported these negroes into this country; you enjoyed the benefits resulting from their carriage and sale; and you reaped the largest profit accruing from the introduction of slaves.

Confederate President Jefferson Davis repeatedly exposed the North's lies and coverups concerning slavery. As a result, he has been completely ignored by pro-North writers for the past century and a half.

FACT 15

AMERICAN BLACK SLAVERY
GOT ITS START IN THE NORTH

Like the American slave trade (which is connected to but is distinct from American slavery), American slavery also got its start as a legal institution in the North. Its birthplace was, of course, none other than Massachusetts, the very *first* of the original 13 states (colonies) to legalize it in 1641. In contrast, the *last* of the original 13 colonies to legalize slavery was a Southern one, Georgia, which officially sanctioned it 108 years later, in 1749.[21]

In Boston, Massachusetts, the cradle of American slavery, a white slave owner (far right) has sold one of his male slaves to a fellow slaveholder in Providence, Rhode Island. The unfortunate father (carrying his few belongings in a wooden box) is saying goodbye to his wife and children for the last time, as friends mourn in the background. Contrary to Yankee myth, the separation of slave families was a common occurrence in the Old North, but rare and even illegal in the Old South.

FACT 16

THE AMERICAN ABOLITION MOVEMENT WAS LAUNCHED IN THE SOUTH

While Northern colonies like Massachusetts were busy legalizing slavery and expanding the slave trade, Southern colonies—who considered anything connected to human bondage as an "evil"—were busy trying to put a stop to both.

Indeed, America's first voluntary emancipation took place in 1655 in a Southern colony, Virginia,[22] the same state that launched the American abolition movement. This occurred as early as 1753, when Virginia began issuing official statutes in an attempt to block the importation of slaves. In 1732, when English military officer James Edward Oglethorpe founded the Southern colony of Georgia, it became the first to place a prohibition against commercial trafficking in slaves into her state constitution, calling the institution "unjust and cruel." North Carolina and South Carolina both passed restrictions on the trade in 1787, as did Tennessee in 1805.

In point of fact, at one time or another *all* of the antebellum Southern states tried to stop both the importation of slaves and the kidnaping and selling of slaves within their borders. In other words, the reality is that *up until the year 1800, nearly all Southerners were abolitionists.*

As all of this was transpiring, the Northern states were busy bringing in as many African slaves as possible through their seaports. In 1776 alone, for example, the year the Declaration of Independence was issued, New Hampshire imported 627 slaves; Massachusetts imported 3,500; Rhode Island, 4,376; Connecticut, 6,000; New Jersey, 7,600; Delaware, 9,000; New York, 15,000; and Maryland, 80,000.

In 1835, when Yankee tourist, Professor Ethan Allen Andrews, told a Virginia slave owner that "the whole public sentiment of the North is decidedly opposed to slavery," the man replied sharply: "So also is that of the South, with but a few exceptions." After visiting the South in the early 1800s, British-American scientist George William Featherstonhaugh wrote:

> All Christian men must unite in the wish that slavery was extinguished in every part of the world, and *from my personal knowledge of the sentiments of many of the leading gentlemen in the Southern States, I am persuaded that they look to the ultimate abolition of slavery with satisfaction.*[23]

There were a number of good reasons for the near universal abolitionism across Dixie:

> At the South . . . humanitarianism though of positive weight was but one of several factors. The distinctively *Southern considerations against the trade* were that its continuance would lower the prices of slaves already on hand, or at least prevent those prices from rising; that it would so increase the staple exports as to spoil the world's market for them; that it would drain out money and keep the community in debt; that *it would retard the civilization of the negroes already on hand*; and that by raising the proportion of blacks in the population it would intensify the danger of slave insurrections.[24]

Of the 130 abolition societies established before 1827 by Northern abolitionist Benjamin Lundy, over 100, comprising four-fifths of the total membership, were in the South. Southern Quakers were among the first to protest the spread of the institution. Other Southerners of note who came out against the "peculiar institution" were Bishop William Meade, Nathaniel Macon, Samuel Doak, Gideon Blackburn, John Rankin, David Nelson, James H. Dickey, James Gilliland, Samuel Crothers, Dyer Burgess, James Lemen, Edward Coles, William T. Allan, James A. Thome, William Ladd, James G. Birney, Christopher Gadsden (designer of the Gadsden Flag), and George Bourne, cofounder of the "American Anti-Slavery Society" in 1833.

America's most famous early Southern abolitionists included George Washington, Patrick Henry, James Madison, St. George Tucker, and Thomas Jefferson, the latter whose complaints regarding Britain's laws forcing slavery on the original 13 colonies helped lead to the American Revolution.[25]

FACT 17

AMERICA'S FIRST KNOWN LEGAL
SLAVE OWNER WAS A BLACK MAN

America's first known official slave owner was Anthony Johnson, an Angolan who came to the colonies as a black African servant. After his arrival in 1621, he worked off his term of indenture and began purchasing human chattel in Virginia, where he accrued great wealth and a large plantation. Later, in the chronicles of Northampton County, there is record of a suit brought by Johnson "for the purpose of recovering his negro servant."

This being the first case of its kind, Johnson, who owned both black *and* white slaves, actually helped launch the American slave trade by forcing authorities to legally define the meaning of "slave ownership." In 1652 his son John Johnson imported and bought eleven white slaves, who worked under him at his Virginia plantation, located on the banks of the Pungoteague River.[26]

America's first official slave owner was a wealthy African, Anthony Johnson, who owned black and white slaves and a large plantation in Virginia.

FACT 18

NEW YORK WAS FOUNDED TO SERVE AS A SLAVE STATE & NEW YORK CITY WAS FOUNDED TO SERVE AS A SLAVE PORT

Originally known as New Amsterdam, New York City grew to become the center of the Dutch colony of what was then called New Netherland (later renamed New York by the English), a territory founded in 1624 and governed by the great slave trading corporation, the Dutch West India Company, whose primary goal was to "extend the market for its human merchandise whithersoever its influence reached."

Fact: New York state was founded as a slave colony, New York City was founded as a slave port.

Today New York City's official flag still bears the colors of the original flag flown by Netherland's slave ships: blue, orange, and white.

Thus it was that slavery took root in New York at the very beginning, when it was established by the Dutch in 1624. This marked the start of the official recognition of slavery in the middle colonies, where the institution quickly became a "custom" in the region.

The location of New York state, and more importantly, New York City, was not accidental. The Dutch had carefully and intentionally chosen them, not only for their many protected inlets, but also for their strategic positions, situated midway between the Northern and Southern colonies. From here they hoped to maximize slave sales and further spread their slave trading business throughout the Eastern seaboard.[27]

FACT 19

New York City was America's Slaving Capital for Over a Century

By the time the slavery-obsessed English took over the colony of New Netherland in 1664 and renamed it New York, it "contained more slaves in proportion to its inhabitants than Virginia." From then on the institution only increased. Between 1697 and 1790, for example, Albany's slave population grew from 3 percent to 16 percent. Influential Albany plantation owners, like the Schuyler and Van Rensselaer families, made vast fortunes using black slaves to build up their estates. A number of their well-known homes stand in New York's capital city to this day, including Ten Broeck Manor, Cherry Hill Mansion, and the Schuyler Mansion.

In 1665 New York passed Duke's Laws, named after the Duke of York (who later became King James II). A codification of statutes borrowed from the Massachusetts Fundamentals (a set of early colonial laws), they allowed Indians and blacks who had not been baptized into the Christian religion to be enslaved.

By the year 1700 New York Harbor was teeming with slave ships and slavery had become the foundation of the state's economy. New Yorkers believed that their "peculiar institution" was so vital to the North's economy that they blocked and delayed emancipation for over 100 years, with so-called "official abolition" not occurring until 1827. New York's slave owners were a brutal lot, engaging in a myriad of cruel practices, from disenfranchisement and the separation of slave families to whipping, torture, and murder.

By the year 1720 New York had become one of the largest slaveholding states in the North, with 4,000 slaves against a white population of only 31,000. The situation was unbearable to the North's few abolitionists, resulting in the nation's first antislavery essay: *The*

Selling of Joseph, penned in Massachusetts by the famed Yankee judge who presided at the Salem witch trials, Samuel Sewall. As in ancient Africa, Israel, and Thrace, slaves were such a valuable commodity in the American North that they could be used as an insurance policy to cover their master's financial obligations, or be sold to pay off the owner's creditors. This led to the illegal Northern practice of falsely claiming free blacks as "personal property," then selling them to pay off debts.

By the mid 1700s one-sixth of New York City's population was comprised of African slaves. By 1756 New York state possessed some 13,000 adult black slaves, giving it the dubious distinction of having the largest slave force of any Northern colony at the time. That same year slaves accounted for 25 percent of the population in Kings, Queens, Richmond, New York City, and Westchester, making these areas the primary bastion of American slavery throughout the rest of the colonial period.

New Englanders moving south to Westchester and Long Island were among the most eager slave purchasers, and by 1750 at least one-tenth of the province of New York's householders were slave owners. At New York City's peak, at least one-fifth of the town's population were slaves. Little wonder that in 1785 New York's state legislators rejected a bill advocating gradual emancipation. In 1860 alone it has been estimated that 85 vessels—all which had been fitted out in and which had sailed from New York City—brought as many as 60,000 African slaves into the U.S.

What Northern and New South historians will not tell you is that there is only one reason that New York City is today America's largest and wealthiest municipality: for centuries it served as the literal heart of North America's slaving industry. Some of the most famous New York names, in fact—names such as the Lehman Brothers, John Jacob Astor, Junius and Pierpont Morgan, Charles Tiffany, Archibald Gracie, and many others—are only known today because of the tremendous riches their families made from the town's highly profitable business.

Many of the 21st-Century's wealthiest New York Jewish families descend from 18th-Century Jewish slave ship owners and slave traders, who eagerly participated with Northern colonial Christians in the Yankee's "peculiar institution."[28]

FACT 20

NEW YORK PRACTICED SLAVERY LONGER THAN ANY OTHER STATE

New York City, the center of America's cotton business as early as 1815, was so deeply connected to the Yankee slave trade and to Southern slavery that it opposed all early attempts at abolition within its borders, and, along with New Jersey, was the last Northern state to resist the passage of emancipation laws.

Being America's slave state capital, it is not surprising that New York practiced slavery for an astonishing 239 years:

1. Slavery in New York officially began (on the island of Manhattan) under the Dutch, and lasted for 38 years, from 1626 to 1664.
2. New York slavery then fell under the auspices of the English, lasting for 112 years, from 1664 to 1776.
3. After the formation of the U.S., New York slavery was turned over to the new state government, continuing on for another 51 years, from 1776 to 1827, when it was legally "abolished."
4. Slavery in New York then persisted illegally for another 38 years, only being permanently shut down by the ratification of the Thirteenth Amendment in December 1865.

New York's 239-year history of slavery is the longest of any state, and certainly far longer than any Southern state. It is greater even than Massachusetts, where both the American slave trade and American slavery got their start. This makes New York America's premier slave state, our one and only true slavocracy, prompting one early historian to refer to the Empire State as a slave "regime never paralleled in equal volume elsewhere."[29]

FACT 21

18ᵀᴴ-CENTURY NORTHERN STATES PROHIBITED EMANCIPATION & IMPOSED LIFELONG SLAVERY ON AFRICAN-AMERICANS

In keeping with their stringent Black Codes (laws designed to restrict the rights of black Americans), in the 1700s New England made manumissions illegal, while in most Northern states, such as New York, slaves were made slaves for life, with no chance of purchasing their freedom.[30]

America's Black Codes, of course, got their start in the Northern states, where American slavery itself was born in the 1600s. Unlike in the South, Yankee slavery laws were the harshest in the country, making Africans slaves for life, with no possibility of freedom through self-purchase.

FACT 22

In 1776 the Northern States Had More Slaves than the South

In 1776, at the time of the formation of the *first* Confederate States of America, the U.S.A., of the 500,000 slaves in the 13 colonies, 300,000 (or 60 percent) were possessed by the Northern ones, only 200,000 (or 40 percent) by the Southern ones. It was only later, when Yankee slave traders pushed slavery south, that Dixie came to possess more slaves than the North.[31]

Up until the early 1800s, the Northern states possessed the majority of America's slaves. It was only then, when slavery became unprofitable and the overwhelming numbers of blacks unbearable to him, that the racist Yankee began phasing out slavery and pushing the institution southward.

FACT 23

THE PERCENTAGE OF YANKEE SLAVE OWNERS WAS ALWAYS HIGHER THAN SOUTHERN ONES

By 1690, in Perth Amboy, New Jersey, as just one example of the Northern colonies, nearly every white inhabitant owned one or more black slaves, and by 1775, 12 percent of the population of eastern New Jersey was comprised of slaves.

A white New England family being served by two black slaves. Percentage wise, there were always more slave owners in the North than in the South.

This means that almost 100 percent of the whites in some Northern cities were slaveholders.

Other Northern states shared similar statistics from this time period. Records from the early 1700s reveal that 42 percent of all New York households owned slaves, and that the share of slaves in both New York and New Jersey was larger than that of North Carolina.

Contrast all of this with the Old South, where at no time did white slave owners make up more than 4.8 percent of the total population (only 25 percent of Southern households possessed one or more slaves), the peak number in 1860. *And as one moves further back in time these figures sharply decrease.* In fact, in most Southern towns there were no slave owners.

The conclusion? The percentage of slaveholders in the Old North was always much higher than slaveholders in the Old South. Do not be fooled by anti-South writers who tell you otherwise.[32]

FACT 24

YANKEES REGISTERED THEIR SLAVES AS "LIVESTOCK," SOUTHERNERS AS FAMILY MEMBERS

From early American records it is quite apparent that Northerners had far less regard for their African-American slaves than Southerners. For instance, the Massachusetts general court evaluated both red and black slaves as "private property" suitable for exportation as "merchandise," while Rhode Island and New Hampshire more specifically taxed them as "livestock."

Northern slaveholders, like this one, registered their slaves as "livestock"; Southern slaveholders registered them as "family members," a fact never noted by our Northern-biased historians.

New Jersey and Pennsylvania—the latter state where blacks were present even before William Penn's colony was founded—preferred to see their slaves as assessable possessions, while New York evaluated its slaves using a poll tax. Everywhere across the North, in fact, black slaves were registered by Yankee families on the same lists as their horses, cattle, tools, kitchen goods, and other common farm and household items.

How different from the South, where slaves were civilly registered as literal members of the families of their white, black, red, or brown owners, and, in nearly all cases, stringently cared for throughout their entire lives, very much as if they were the adopted children of their masters. Little wonder that many Southern blacks did not welcome emancipation, preferring servitude instead.[33]

FACT 25

IN 1787 THE NEW ENGLAND STATES VOTED TO KEEP THE AFRICAN SLAVE TRADE OPEN FOR AS LONG AS POSSIBLE

When New England abolitionist William Lloyd Garrison campaigned for the secession of the Northern states from the Union, so that they could break their association with the "horrid slave states" to the South, another Yankee "antislavery reformer," Henry Ward Beecher, disagreed, saying:

> . . . Union with slaveholders was not a sound principle of political action [on which the North could secede]. [New England] secession from the Union was neither right nor expedient. It was not right, because the North as well as the South was responsible for the existence of slavery; the North as well as the South had entertained and maintained it; *the importation of slaves was carried on by New England shipping merchants and defended by New England representatives; and when the proposition came before the Constitutional Convention [in 1787] for the prohibition of the slave-trade, New England voted for the clause that it should not be abolished until 1808. Thus the North shared with the South in the responsibility for the sin and shame of slavery*, and it had no right, Pilate-like, to wash its hands and say, "We are guiltless of this matter." It was under sacred obligation to remain in the partnership and work for the renovation of the nation. As it was not right, so neither was it expedient.[34]

The Northern states were so heavily invested in the slave trade that they did not completely relinquish it until they were forced to in 1865.

FACT 26

IN THE 1800S MANY NORTHERN STATES BANNED BLACK SUFFRAGE

The legal prohibition of black suffrage "was imposed by numerous Northern states between 1807 and 1838," an idea that quickly spread across Yankeedom at the time. This particular form of white Yankee racism in and around Washington, D.C. carried on well into the Grant administration, as English tourist Henry Latham noted in 1867:

The two Houses having passed a bill that every coloured man who had resided for one year in the district of Columbia should possess the suffrage, sent it up to the President [Grant], who returned it to-day with his veto, assigning his reasons. The chief reasons assigned were: that although Congress does constitutionally make State laws for the district of Columbia, yet they are not representatives elected by that district; that *a vote had recently been taken of the white citizens of the district, and they had almost unanimously refused the suffrage to the negroes; that the effect of the bill would be to alter the constitution of the district against the expressed wish of its citizens, and would result in its being filled with negroes coming in from the surrounding States.*[35]

Northern laws prohibiting blacks from voting continued on after Lincoln's War, and even after slave owner and Union General Ulysses S. Grant became U.S. president.

FACT 27

THE NORTH, NOT THE SOUTH, LAUNCHED BOTH THE AMERICAN SLAVE TRADE & AMERICAN SLAVERY

In 1638 Massachusetts instigated the American slave trade when Boston began importing African slaves commercially for the first time. This occurred when Captain William Pierce brought New

A slave auction in Boston, Massachusetts, birthplace of both the American slave trade and American slavery.

England's first remunerative shipload of Africans from the West Indies aboard the 120-ton Salem vessel *Desire*, built at Marblehead, Massachusetts, in 1636.

Just three years later, in 1641, Massachusetts gave birth to American slavery when it became the first colony to legitimatize and monetize the institution. By 1676 Boston slavers were routinely coming home with shiploads of human cargo from East Africa and Madagascar. By 1775 Massachusetts had over 5,000 black slaves and 30,000 bondservants.[36]

FACT 28

THERE WERE FEW LAWS PROTECTING SLAVES IN THE NORTHERN STATES

Yankee slave owners had complete freedom to discipline their chattel in any manner they saw fit, and various barbarities—from whipping and branding, to public torture and burning slaves at the stake—were legal, routine, and socially accepted.

In New York, for example, where a 1702 law authorized masters to chastise their human property at their own discretion, slaves convicted of heinous crimes, such as murder, were subject to all manner of hideous fates. These included being "burned at the stake," "gibbeted alive," and "broken on the wheel." This is precisely what

New York families relishing a routine public slave execution. This black man is being burned at the stack for a crime under one of the North's ultra racist and strict slave laws.

occurred in 1712, when New York authorities hanged 13 slaves, burned four of them alive (one over a "slow fire"), "broke" one on the wheel, and left another to starve to death chained to the floor. In 1741 alone the Empire State executed 31 blacks: 13 were burned at the stake, 18 were hanged, while another 71 were transported out of state. On another occasion a New York slave named Tom, found guilty of killing two people, was ordered to be "roasted over a slow fire so that he will suffer in torment for at least eight to ten hours." Such executions were performed in public, in full view of ordinary New Yorkers.[37]

FACT 29

THERE WERE NUMEROUS LAWS PROTECTING
SLAVES IN THE SOUTHERN STATES

In the Old South black servants were protected by a literal bible of hundreds of rigorous rules and regulations, crimes against slaves were punishable by law, and cruel slaveholders, though rare, were harshly penalized (even executed) when caught. The result was that the vast majority of Southern slaves lived lives of comfort, safety, health, and security from birth to death—which is why so many of them, when given a choice, preferred servitude to emancipation.

In 1900 Dr. Henry A. White, history professor at Washington and Lee University, made the following astute comments; words that should be permanently enshrined in granite in the capitol building of every Southern state:

> The [Southern slavery] system produced no paupers and no orphans; food and clothing the negro did not lack; careful attention he received in sickness, and, without a burden [care] the aged servants spent their closing days. The plantation was an industrial school where the negro gradually acquired skill in the use of tools. A bond of affection was woven between Southern masters and servants which proved strong enough in 1861-'65 to keep the negroes at voluntary labour to furnish food for the armies that contended against [Lincoln's] military emancipation.[38] In the planter's home the African learned to set a higher value upon the domestic virtues which he saw illustrated in the lives of Christian men and women; for, be it remembered, the great body of the slave-holders of the South were devotees of the religious faith handed down through pious ancestors from [John] Knox, [Thomas] Cranmer, [John] Wesley, and [John] Bunyan. With truth, perhaps, it may be said than no other economic system before or since that time has engendered a bond of personal affection between capital and labour so strong as that established by the institution of slavery.[39]

FACT 30

WHEN GIVEN A CHOICE BLACK AMERICAN SLAVES PREFERRED TO BE OWNED BY SOUTHERN SLAVEHOLDERS OVER NORTHERN ONES

Unlike in the North, in the South slaves were paid a weekly salary and were given Sundays, rainy days, and holidays off. Southern servants were also permitted time to hunt, fish, and visit loved ones on neighboring farms and plantations. On Saturdays, the day traditionally set aside for Southern servants to work their own land, they labored either a half day, or had the entire day free. Each year they also had several week's worth of work free holidays (such as Christmas, Good Friday, Independence

When polled, both Northern and Southern slaves said that they would much prefer being owned by a Southern slaveholder than a Northern slaveholder. This obviously contented, well-paid, cheerful Southern house servant is enjoying a few moments with his easy-going "master," a 19th-Century Tennessee planter.

Day, and the post harvest period), with odd days off as rewards. On many plantations there was a servant-only party held every Saturday night, complete with whiskey, a barbeque, music (items often contributed by the white owners), and dancing. Southern slaves worked from sunrise to early afternoon (eight hours) five days a week, with one to three hours off for lunch. Thus their average work week was 25 to 40 hours long, far below the 75 hour work week of free whites and blacks at the time. The life of the Southern slave was indeed easy and secure compared to the far more difficult life of the Yankee slave. This is why, when asked, nearly 100 percent of American blacks said they would rather be owned by a Southern slaveholder than a Northern one.[40]

FACT 31

FOREIGN VISITORS TO THE U.S. TESTIFIED THAT LIFE WAS MUCH WORSE FOR ENGLISH LABORERS THAN FOR SOUTHERN SLAVES

After living in the American South for several years, for instance, Scotsman William Thomson favorably compared agricultural slavery to the industrial slavery experienced by the millions of free white "wage slaves" working in the world's factories and mines:

> *I have seen children in factories, both in England and Scotland, under ten years of age, working twelve hours a-day, till their little hands were bleeding. I have seen these children whipped, when their emaciated limbs could no longer support them to their work; and I believe there is not a planter in America whose blood would not rise, and whose arm would not be lifted up to defend even the negroes from such cruelty; especially the native [Southern] planter, who is much better to his negroes than the planters that have been brought up in free [Northern] states. This is an acknowledged fact, and therefore I need not illustrate it.* If I were to look for the cause of the comparative kindly feeling of the native [Southern] planter, it would partly be found in his *having been nursed and tended in infancy by some careful negro, and having made playmates of the little black fellows of his father's house.* I acknowledge that the miserably degraded state of the [white] factory slave, or the equally unnatural condition of the [white] miners, is no apology for the continuance of negro slavery; and I only make the comparison to show how difficult it is, under the present irrational state of society, to render pleasant the condition of the "hewers of wood and drawers of water." *I consider myself in some degree qualified to make this comparison, for I have witnessed negro slavery in mostly all the slave-holding states in America; having lived for weeks on cotton plantations, observing closely the actual condition of the negroes; and can assert, without fear of contradiction from any man who has any knowledge of the subject, that I have never witnessed one-fifth of the real suffering that I have seen in manufacturing establishments in Great Britain.*[41]

FACT 32

ANTILITERACY SLAVE LAWS WERE A CREATION OF THE LIBERAL NORTH NOT THE CONSERVATIVE SOUTH

Antiliteracy laws, meant to prevent both black slaves and free blacks from learning to read and write, were first invented in the puritanical North, where they were strictly and sometimes violently enforced.

As hard evidence for the widespread existence of antiliteracy sentiment, not to mention overt white racism, in the North prior to Lincoln's War, we need look no further than the doleful story of Prudence Crandall.

Crandall was a white New England teacher who founded the "High School for Young Colored Ladies and Misses" in Canterbury, Connecticut, in 1834. One would think that fellow Yanks, had they—as we have been taught—been true non-racist egalitarians, would have applauded her efforts. Instead, for trying to offer blacks a free education in New England, Crandall, a Quaker and abolitionist, was harassed, persecuted, arrested (three times), imprisoned, and had her home burned down, while Northern white mobs attacked and stoned her school, tore it from its foundations using a team of 100 oxen, then physically drove her out of the state.

None of Connecticut's white population shed a tear for Crandall. Instead, the state, and in particular her politicians, were quite happy to see her, and her school, disappear. Their parting comment perfectly sums up the North's feelings about blacks and black education during this period: "Once open this door, and New-England will become the Liberia of America," they shrieked as Crandall left Connecticut for the final time. New Hampshire whites followed suit by destroying their state's own all-black schools.[42]

FACT 33

WHEN ANTILITERACY-LAWS AROSE DECADES LATER IN THE MORE LENIENT SOUTH, THEY WERE HABITUALLY DISREGARDED BY SERVANT OWNERS, THE CONSTABULARY, & THE SOUTHERN JUDICIAL SYSTEM

After they arose in the North, antiliteracy laws did eventually make their way South. However, in opposition to Yankee propaganda, they were never enacted in "all" of the Southern states. Actually, only four Southern states ever bothered to ratify such statues: Virginia, Georgia, North Carolina, and South Carolina, and even here they were loosely obeyed and routinely disregarded. Kentucky and Tennessee never issued them, and the rest of the Southern states simply ignored the entire issue since it was both inhumane and illogical.

Antiliteracy laws in the South were repeatedly ignored by both slave owners and the law, and, in fact, most masters encouraged their servants to learn to read and write.

The fact is that, just as famed Southern diarist Mary Chesnut did, millions of Southern slave owners intentionally taught their servants to read and write; or just as often the servants taught themselves. Thus the Northern myth that slave owners prevented their servants from becoming literate for fear of them becoming "too smart," "impudent," and "uppity" is just that, a Northern myth—certainly true of ancient Rome, but completely false when it came to the Victorian American South.[43]

FACT 34

JIM CROW LAWS WERE "UNIVERSAL" IN ALL OF THE NORTHERN STATES, BUT RARE & "UNUSUAL" IN THE OLD SOUTH

Wherever the various races have the least amount of contact, racism tends to increase—no matter what the skin color of the dominant or majority race.

And this is precisely the situation we find in the Old South and the Old North, for in the latter region most whites had little if any interaction with blacks, making racism far more ingrained. Thus we find that Jim Crow laws, along with both legal and customary segregation, for instance, were "universal" in all of the Northern states, but were "unusual" in the South.[44]

The Old South was an interracial society with few anti-black laws. This discouraged racism while inducing warm relations between whites and blacks. The opposite was true in the Old North.

FACT 35

SEGREGATION WAS THE NORM IN THE OLD NORTH, BUT COMPLETELY UNKNOWN IN THE ANTEBELLUM SOUTH

Since Jim Crow laws in the South were scarce (and seldom enforced where they existed), it is not surprising that racial segregation was also rare. In fact, during the antebellum period there is not a single known case of segregation anywhere in Dixie. Conversely, it was endemic to America's northeastern states right up to, and far beyond, the 1860s.

There was no segregation in the Old South, and relationships between the races were typically mutually affectionate, respectful, and friendly—just as they are in the South to this day.

The North's onerous Black Codes forbade, among many other things, black immigration and black civil rights, and even banned blacks from attending public schools. Little wonder that those blacks who managed to survive in the North were generally less educated and less skilled than Southern blacks. Up to 1855 it was this very type of oppression that prevented blacks from serving as jurors in all but one Northern state: Massachusetts.

Even after Lincoln's fake and illegal Final Emancipation Proclamation was issued (on January 1, 1863), literally nothing changed for African-Americans living north of the Mason-Dixon Line. When former slaves managed to make economic progress there, they found themselves blocked at every turn by a hostile racist Northern government, the very body that had "emancipated" them. As mentioned, this blockage was accomplished not only by Black Codes, by also through the implementation of severe Jim Crow laws and public segregation laws, both which were unconditionedly and widely supported by the Yankee populace.[45]

FACT 36

ANTEBELLUM BLACKS WHO TRIED TO MOVE TO OR WORK IN THE NORTH, IN PARTICULAR ILLINOIS, WERE ARRESTED & ENSLAVED

While on the topic of our sixteenth president and Northern racism, we should point out that "The Land of Lincoln," Illinois, Lincoln's adopted home state, was one of the most anti-black, pro-Jim Crow states in America at the time. This was, in large part, because of his work to restrict black civil rights there, rights which he dismissed as mere "false issues." White Illinoisans, for example, arguably among the most racist Northerners in the 1850s and 60s, threatened to start "a war of extermination" if blacks were given equal rights in their state. It was said that Illinois' Black Codes were so severe that the civil rights of African-Americans were "virtually nonexistent" in the Prairie State. Thus it was that Massachusetts Governor Edward Everett once described the condition of "free" blacks in the North as one of "disability, discouragement, and hardship." And here is proof.

In the early 1800s a group of 19 free blacks were so despondent over the treatment they received from whites in Illinois that they penned a letter to the state's chapter of the American Colonization Society, begging to be transported to the African colony of Liberia. Their desperation was so great that they even offered themselves as lifelong slaves to the ACS in exchange for ship fare.

English abolitionist Marshall Hall visited the U.S. in the mid 1800s, and discovered, to his horror, a thriving racial bigotry among Northern whites—especially Illinois whites—one he aptly termed "the second slavery." Writes Hall:

> In some of the States, termed free, in Ohio, in Indiana, but

especially in Illinois, [the black man] . . . is absolutely prohibited and excluded by State-law, and by recent State-law too, from taking up his abode and pursuing some humble calling of industry. *If he attempt to do so, he is actually driven, or sold, from the state, re-sold into slavery!* What words can adequately characterize such legislation? . . . What a contrast does this Illinois present with Old England! In England, the moment the slave's foot touches the soil, he is free. *In Illinois, the moment the free-man of colour touches the soil, of his own country too, even the country of his birth, he becomes—an alien, or—a slave!*[46]

In 1862, Lincoln, who as an attorney had once defended a slave owner in court (and lost), helped the citizens of Illinois amend their state constitution to include a passage that read, "no negro or mulatto shall immigrate or settle in this state." He even urged the Illinois legislature to set aside funding to deport all free blacks from the state in order to prevent *miscegenation* (that is, racial interbreeding), a racist word invented, not by Southerners, but by Northerners.

With men like Lincoln serving in its government it is certainly no surprise that Illinois was so anti-black. After all, it was Old Abe himself who, on July 17, 1858, made a public speech at Springfield, Illinois, that included the following words: "What I would most desire would be the separation of the white and black races."

In 1857 Lincoln aided in the white supremacist movement in his state by asking the Illinois legislature to appropriate funds for the deportation of all blacks out of the state. Why? As just noted, to help prevent one of his greatest fears: the dilution of the white race through interracial reproduction.

Whites from central Illinois in particular had little use for blacks, considering them, not human beings, but lowly creatures, little more than livestock "with wool on their heads." Wrote one newspaper editor from the area, who could not abide the idea of free blacks moving to Illinois: "We don't want any Negroes around here. Send them all to the Northeast!"

An Illinois senator, Joseph Kitchell, was of the same mind as the rest of the whites in his state, including Lincoln. The residence of Negroes among us, he announced, *even as servants . . . is productive of moral and political evil. . . . The natural difference between them and ourselves forbids the idea that they should ever be permitted to participate with us in the political affairs of our government.*[47]

Illinoisans passed countless anti-integration and anti-immigration laws to prevent blacks from settling in or even traveling through their state, with punishments ranging from whipping to being sold back into slavery at public auction. In 1862 Illinois voters adopted a constitutional provision that barred the further admission of blacks into their state, a Black Code that Lincoln allowed to remain on the books until 1865, the year his War finally came to an end. In 1863, for instance, eight blacks were arrested and convicted for entering Illinois unlawfully. Of these, seven were sold back into slavery (temporarily) to pay off their fines—all under Lincoln's watch.

Before and even after Lincoln's War, Southern blacks seeking to live and work in the Northern states were subjected to both white racism and a myriad of anti-black laws, from simple fines and imprisonment to deportation and even enslavement. Former Northern slave Frederick Douglass, as just one example, could not find work as a caulker in Massachusetts due to the color of his skin.

Even after the War white Illinoisans continued to heavily discriminate against blacks. One postbellum Illinois law required that free blacks possess a "certificate of freedom" and post a bond of $1,000 to reside in the state. Those who violated these conditions were subject to arrest, after which they were hired out as a laborer (what Yankees would call a slave) for one year.[48]

FACT 37

NORTHERN BLACKS WHO MARRIED NORTHERN WHITE WOMEN WERE SOLD INTO PERMANENT SLAVERY

Illinois was far from being the only Northern state that feared "race-mixing," or which issued these types of severe Black Codes. Massachusetts had some of the most exacting anti-miscegenation rules on the books. Blacks convicted of violating New England's racist puritanical laws were sold and deported, usually to the West Indies, where they faced a life of bitter toil on England's sprawling sugar plantations. Massachusetts, New Jersey, Pennsylvania, and Connecticut all approved of castration as another means of "curing" black males of intermingling with white females, and also as a punishment for rape or even attempted rape of white females.

Northern blacks who violated the Yankee's many rigorous anti-black laws faced brutal punishments and tortures that included whipping, castration, enslavement, and deportation.

Like Massachusetts, Pennsylvania passed unsparing laws against interracial "mixing." A 1726 statute upheld the longtime custom of punishing free blacks who had relations with white women by forcing them into slavery for seven years. Any African-American, free or enslaved, who married a white female was to be forced into slavery for life.[49]

FACT 38

NEW YORK WAS ONE OF THE MOST RACIST OF THE NORTHERN STATES

Naturally, New York City, America's slavery capital for decades, had its own set of strict Black Codes, all which were considered particularly savage by humanitarians and abolitionists. Offences by black servants could garner punishments ranging from beatings and whippings to expatriation and even execution. In 1741 the mere hint of a slave revolt resulted in the public killing of 27 Northern slaves, all who were either hanged or burned at the stake.

White New Yorkers as a whole were arguably the most racially intolerant of any of the Northern states, perhaps second only to the citizens of Illinois and Massachusetts. This is certainly why, for instance, New York City had far less black artisans than Southern towns, such as the far more racially tolerant New Orleans. Between 1702 and 1741 alone the Empire State passed a massive series of statutes that, among other things, allowed blacks convicted of heinous acts to be executed "in such a manner as the enormity of their crimes might be deemed to merit." Along with this law manumissions were restricted, free New York blacks were prohibited from holding real estate, and the state's entire set of Black Codes was strengthened in an effort to gain greater control over both slaves and blacks in general. Well into the 1830s not even free blacks were allowed to drive their own hacks or carts. This same law was also active in Baltimore, Maryland, while in Philadelphia, Pennsylvania, free blacks were not allowed to drive an omnibus.

Hundreds of such illustrations from the racist Old North could be given. No wonder so many blacks wanted to get as far away from Yankeedom as they could, requesting that they be sent as far South as possible (to places like New Orleans), or even out of the country.[50]

FACT 39

AUTHENTIC SLAVERY WAS PRACTICED IN THE NORTH, SERVITUDE WAS PRACTICED IN THE SOUTH

Two of the key indicators of *authentic* slavery are that 1) a slave has no rights of any kind, and 2) he or she cannot purchase their freedom. Both of these rights, however, are available under a much milder form of bondage known as servitude, making it completely different than true slavery.

Contrary to the myths of Northern anti-South propagandists, from slavery's first appearance in the South, black servants were accorded a myriad of civil and

In the Old North black bondsmen were known as "slaves" and were enslaved for life. Here they were much more likely to be brutalized, heavily exploited, worked in chains on a rigidly run plantation, and owned by a strict, racist master.

personal rights, and also could purchase their freedom at any time. In fact, the first blacks in the American South came to this country as indentured servants, just as most white colonists did at the time.

The truth is that it was in the colonial North, where there were few laws protecting blacks and where slaves could not buy their liberty, that genuine slavery was practiced. What North and New South writers conveniently and slanderously call Southern "slavery" then was actually, as Edward A. Pollard rightly asserts, a "well-guarded and moderate system of negro servitude." As he wrote during Lincoln's War:

In referring to the condition of the negro in this war, we use the term *"slavery"* . . . under strong protest. For *there is no such thing in the South; it is a term fastened upon us by the exaggeration and conceit of Northern literature*, and most improperly acquiesced in by Southern writers. *There is a system of African servitude in the South; in which the negro, so far from being under the absolute dominion of his master (which is the true meaning of the vile word "slavery"), has, by law of the land, his personal rights recognized and protected, and his comfort and "right" of "happiness" consulted, and by the practice of the system, has a sum of individual indulgences, which makes him altogether the most striking type in the world of cheerfulness and contentment.* And the system of servitude in the South has this peculiarity over other systems of servitude in the world: that it does not debase one of God's creatures from the condition of free-citizenship and membership in organized society and [which] thus rest on acts of debasement and disenfranchisement, but [instead it] elevates a savage, and rests on the solid basis of human improvement. The European mind, adopting the nomenclature of our enemies, has designated as "slavery" what is really *the most virtuous system of servitude in the world*.[51]

In the Old South black "slaves" were known more correctly as "servants" and could purchase their liberty whenever they wished. As this early illustration of a typical tobacco plantation in 1859 shows, here they were much more likely to be well cared-for, possess countless freedoms, live on an informally run plantation, and be owned by a friendly and indulgent master. The North has suppressed these self-evident facts for 150 years.

FACT 40

AS "SLAVES" GO, SOUTHERN BLACKS HAD THE HIGHEST STANDARD OF LIVING IN THE WORLD

Southern servitude functioned much like a social welfare program with built-in, lifelong health care and life insurance, operating in some ways like an early form of socialism. Yes, servants helped defray these costs through their work and through monthly percentage payments to their employers. But they earned wages at the same time as well, both via their regular work and also from their personal extracurricular labors. In all, most Southern slaves were so highly indulged and protected by their owners that *being a "slave" came to be an enviable status symbol among many blacks.* Such bold facts have forced even the most South-loathing, biased historians to admit an obvious truth: *Southern servants were treated far better than servants in any other part of the New World, including the American North.*

Would servile blacks have given all these benefits up for freedom? Some would have, and some certainly did. But, after contemplating the quasi-freedom of living in the North, where the anti-African Black Codes were strictly enforced and where white racism was more deeply entrenched, many Southern blacks reconsidered. When Lincoln's War came, this group, most of whom were third, fourth, and fifth generation Southern-Americans, quite consciously chose to remain in the South, in their own homes, on the plantations with their "white families." Then, when "Honest Abe" freed them, and he and the North tried to deport them back to Africa, with one voice this group cried "no!" For they quite rightly considered themselves true Americans and true Southerners. After all, by 1860, 99 percent of all blacks were native-born Americans, a larger percentage than for whites. Thus former Southern servant Booker T. Washington wrote: "I was born in the South. I have lived and labored in the South. I wish to be buried in the South."[52]

FACT 41

EARLY IRISH IMMIGRANTS WERE TREATED FAR WORSE THAN SOUTHERN "SLAVES"

According to 18th-Century Southerners, Irish immigrants, who often came over as servants or even slaves, were treated much worse than imported African slaves.

One of these eyewitnesses was Henry Laurens, a wealthy South Carolinian rice planter and merchant, and president of the U.S. Confederate Congress (from 1777-1778). Laurens, who eventually got out of the African slave trade business due to its "barbarities," was once suddenly put in charge of several shiploads of Irish Protestants who were imported to his state in 1768. Of this experience he wrote to a friend:

18th-Century Irish slaves being driven to work under the lash.

> If you knew the whole affair it would make your humanity shudder. *I have been largely concerned in the African trade.* I quitted the profits arising from that gainful branch principally because of many acts from the masters and others concerned toward the wretched negroes from the time of purchasing to that of selling them again, some of which, although within my knowledge, were uncontrollable—yet *I never saw an instance of cruelty in ten or twelve years experience in that branch equal to the cruelty exercised upon those poor Irish. . . . Self interest prompted the baptized heathen [Yankee slave ship captains] to take some care of their wretched [African] slaves for a market, but no other care was taken of those poor Protestant Christians from Ireland but to deliver as many as possible alive on shore upon the cheapest terms, no matter how they fared upon the voyage nor in what condition they were landed.*[53]

FACT 42

FEW CONFEDERATE GENERALS OWNED SLAVES & MOST WERE ABOLITIONISTS

The vast majority of Southerners, as well as Confederate militiamen and politicians, were longtime advocates of not only abolition, but of black enlistment as well. One of these was General Robert E. Lee, across the South still one of the most beloved and highly regarded Confederate officers.

On December 27, 1856, five years before Lincoln's War, Lee—who unlike General Grant and many other Northern officers, never owned slaves in the literal or technical sense, and who had always been opposed to slavery—wrote a letter to his wife Mary Anna in which he stated that slavery is a "moral and political evil," worse even for the white race than for the black race.

Lee's sentiment is just what one would expect from a Virginian, the state where the American abolition movement began, and whose native sons, most notably U.S. Presidents George Washington and Thomas Jefferson, struggled for so long to rid America of the institution; and this while the North was sending hundreds of slave ships to Africa, and whose main port cities, like New York, Providence, Philadelphia, Baltimore, and Boston, were functioning as the literal epicenters of slave trading in the Western hemisphere.

But Lee was far from being the first prominent Confederate to advocate emancipation and the recruitment of Southern blacks. Another example was my cousin Confederate General Pierre G. T. Beauregard, the "Hero of Fort Sumter" and co-designer of the Confederate Battle Flag.

Yet another important Southerner was Louisiana governor and commander-in-chief Thomas O. Moore, who, on March 24, 1862, commissioned the first black militia in the Confederacy (the Native

Guards of Louisiana). Moore called on the all-black unit, one that had already been protecting New Orleans for several months, to "maintain their organization, and . . . hold themselves prepared for such orders as may be transmitted to them." Their purpose? To guard homes, property, and Southern rights against "the pollution of a ruthless [Northern] invader."

Another noteworthy pro-black white Confederate officer was General Patrick R. Cleburne, known as the "Stonewall Jackson of the West" for his bold tactics on the battlefield. A native of Ireland and a division commander in the Army of Tennessee, at an officers' meeting on January 2, 1864, the Irishman disclosed a written proposal that would soon become known as the "Cleburne Memorial." Calling for the immediate enlistment and training of black soldiers, it promised complete emancipation for *all* Southern slaves at the end of the War.

In early 1865 Southern Congressman Ethelbert Barksdale stated before the House that *every* Confederate soldier, whatever his rank, wanted and supported black enlistment. This sentiment was backed up by such establishments as the renowned Virginia Military Institute, which agreed, if called upon, to train Southern blacks in the art of soldiering.[54]

Confederate General Robert E. Lee, one of the South's most ardent and longstanding abolitionists.

FACT 43

MANY UNION GENERALS, LIKE ULYSSES S. GRANT, OWNED SLAVES & SAID THEY WOULD NOT FIGHT FOR ABOLITION

Thousands of Yankees are known to have owned slaves right up to and through Lincoln's War. Among them were the families of Union General George H. Thomas, Union Admiral David G. Farragut, Union General Winfield Scott, and the family of Lincoln's wife, Mary Todd.

Arguably the most famous Yankee slaveholder was Union General Ulysses S. Grant, an Ohioan who evinced no sympathy for the situation of American blacks, never discussed the Underground Railroad, and as an officer in the Mexican War, was waited on by servants—one, a Mexican man named Gregorio, whom he took home with him after the War to entertain his family. Grant never showed any personal interest in his colored servants—except perhaps those who attended him while he was slowly dying in New York in 1885.

Upon his marriage to Julia Boggs Dent in 1848, Grant inherited a small army of 30 black Maryland slaves that belonged to her family. Later, in 1858, he was known to still own "three or four slaves, given to his wife by her father," Colonel Frederick Dent. Grant leased several additional slaves and personally purchased at least one, a 35 year old black man named William Jones. Never once did he reveal a desire to free either his own slaves or Julia's. Instead, like his wife, and most other Northerners at the time, Grant assumed that the white race was superior to non-white races, and that this was simply the natural order of things.

On the eve of Lincoln's War in early 1861, Grant grew increasingly excited over the possibility that a conflict with the South would greatly depreciate black labor, then, he happily exclaimed, "the nigger will never disturb this country again." In an 1862 letter to his father, Jesse Root Grant, General Grant wrote honestly:

> I have no hobby of my own with regard to the negro, either to effect his freedom or to continue his bondage.

This apathy for the black man continued throughout Lincoln's War. In 1863 Grant penned: "I never was an abolitionist, not even what could be called anti-slavery." Even after the issuance of Lincoln's Emancipation Proclamation Grant maintained the same sentiment, noting sourly that white Americans were now still "just as free to avoid the social intimacy with the blacks as ever they were . . ."

Like many Union generals, Ulysses S. Grant was a slave owner who said that he would not fight for abolition.

Since Lincoln's bogus and illicit Emancipation Proclamation on January 1, 1863, did not liberate slaves in the North (or anywhere else, for that matter), Grant was permitted to keep his black chattel—which is precisely what he did. In fact, he did not free them until he was forced to by the passage of the Thirteenth Amendment on December 6, 1865, which occurred eight months *after* Lincoln's death and the War had ended.

And what or who was behind the Thirteenth Amendment? It was not Grant, Lincoln, Garrison, or any other Northerner. It was proposed by a *Southern* man, John Henderson of Missouri.

But the amendment seemed to have little meaning to Grant or his wife Julia, the latter, who as late as 1876, still looked upon all blacks as slaves. We should not be shocked by any of this. It was the celebrated Yankee General Grant who, in the midst of Lincoln's War, said that the only purpose of the conflict was to "restore the union," and if he ever found out it was for abolition he would immediately defect to the other side and join the Confederacy.[55]

FACT 44

IN 1860 A MERE 4.8 PERCENT OF SOUTHERNERS OWNED SLAVES

P ro-North writers would have us believe that "every Southerner was once a slave owner." However, the opposite is true. In 1860 the South had reached its highest rate of slave ownership. According to the U.S. Census that year, with a white population of 7,215,525, only 4.8 percent, or 385,000, of all Southerners owned slaves, the other 95.2 percent did not. Of those that did, most owned less than five.

Correcting for the mistakes of Census takers—which would include counting slave-hirers as slave owners and counting more than once those thousands of slave owners who annually moved the same slaves back and forth across multiple states—this figure, 4.8 percent, is no doubt too large. Either way, at the time Southerners themselves believed that only about 5 percent of their number owned slaves, which is slightly high, but roughly accurate.[56]

Contrary to Yankee myth, at slavery's peak in the antebellum South in 1860, only 4.8 percent of white adult males owned black servants. Southern historian Shelby Foote rightly called the other 95.2 percent "the slaveless majority," a phrase never mentioned in pro-North books.

FACT 45

ANTEBELLUM YANKEES VIEWED SLAVERY AS THE "CORNERSTONE OF THE UNION"

Anti-South writers enjoy excoriating Confederate Vice President Alexander H. Stephens for his March 21, 1861, speech at Savannah, Georgia, in which he made this infamous statement:

> [The] corner-stone [of the Constitution of the Southern Confederacy] rests upon the great truth, that the negro is not equal to the white man; that slavery, subordination to the superior race, is his natural and normal condition.

Before discussing the facts behind these words, let us compare them with those of Yankee President Abraham Lincoln, delivered publicly a few years earlier on July 17, 1858, at Springfield, Illinois:

> My declarations upon this subject of negro slavery may be misrepresented, but cannot be misunderstood. *I have said that I do not understand the Declaration [of Independence] to mean that all men were created equal in all respects. . . . Certainly the negro is not our equal in color—perhaps not in many other respects . . .*[57]

A few months later, on September 18, 1858, at Charleston, Illinois, Lincoln made the following statement:

> I will say then that *I am not, nor ever have been, in favor of bringing about in any way the social and political equality of the white and black races—that I am not, nor ever have been, in favor of making voters or jurors of negroes, nor of qualifying them to hold office, nor to intermarry with white people*; and I will say in addition to this that *there is a physical difference between the white and black races which I believe will forever forbid the two races living together on terms of social and political equality.* And inasmuch as they cannot so live, while they do

remain together there must be the position of superior and inferior,
and *I as much as any other man am in favor of having the superior position
assigned to the white race.*[58]

Our point here is that Vice President Stephens' racism was no different
than President Lincoln's. Both men were products of a 19th-Century
white society that saw blacks as an "inferior race," as Lincoln *always*
referred to African-Americans. Thus, if critics of the South wish to avoid
being called hypocrites, Northerner Lincoln must be denounced just as
heartily as Southerner Stephens. As the "Great Emancipator" Lincoln
himself said of "nearly all white people" living in America at the time:

> There is a natural disgust in the minds of nearly all white people, to the
> idea of an indiscriminate amalgamation of the white and black races.[59]

As for Stephens' words, they turn out to be far less vicious and
racist than modern South-loathers have asserted—and in fact Stephens
was widely known as a true friend of the black man.[60] For one thing, the
Vice President was engaging in hyperbole to get his point across, a
common enough practice among politicians. Second, the speech we read
today is not a literal translation of the original, but an "interpretation" by
journalists in the audience, who introduced their own biases and
mistakes into the final transcription. Third, Stephens himself repeatedly
maintained that his words were misinterpreted, and for good reason.
When he made his comment about slavery being the "cornerstone" of
American society, he was merely repeating the words of a *Yankee* judge,
Associate Justice of the U.S. Supreme Court, Henry Baldwin of
Connecticut who, 28 years earlier, in 1833, had said:

> *Slavery is the corner-stone of the [U.S.] Constitution.* The foundations
> of the Government are laid and rest on the rights of property in
> slaves, and the whole structure must fall by disturbing the corner-
> stone.[61]

As Richard M. Johnston noted later in 1884, all Stephens did during his
"Cornerstone Speech" was accurately point out the fact that "on the
subject of slavery there was no essential change in the new [Southern
Confederate] Constitution from the old [the U.S. Constitution]."[62]

FACT 46

THE NORTH PRACTICED SLAVERY FOR OVER A CENTURY LONGER THAN THE SOUTH

Southern slavery lasted from 1749, when Georgia became the first Southern state to legalize slavery, to 1865, the year the Thirteenth Amendment was ratified and American slavery was officially abolished, a mere 116 years.

In contrast, Northern slavery lasted from 1641, when Massachusetts became the first Northern state to legalize slavery, to 1865, a span of 224 years. This period increases if we count from 1626, the year New York imported the first black slaves into North America, a span of 239 years—ending in 1865.

Either way, the North practiced slavery for over a century longer than the South did, between 108 and 123 years longer.[63]

The Northern states engaged in slavery over 100 years longer than the Southern states. In this illustration a Yankee slave ship from Rhode Island sits at anchor off the coast of West Africa, while on shore hired hands brand freshly purchased slaves (already previously enslaved by native Africans). The South never engaged in the slave trade, legalized slavery long *after* the North, and sought abolition long *before* the North.

FACT 47

THE MOST DANGEROUS LEG OF AN AFRICAN SLAVE'S JOURNEY WAS NOT THE MIDDLE PASSAGE BUT THE BEGINNING PASSAGE

While there is no doubt that the Middle Passage was indeed horrendous in many ways, it was not the most hazardous or unpleasant leg of an African slave's journey through the notorious Slave Triangle, as pro-North writers insist. It was the harrowing Beginning Passage, the land route from Africa's interior to the coast, where three times as many slaves died as on the Middle Passage.

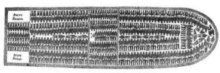

With all of its horrors, the European controlled Middle Passage was not the worst leg of a slave's journey. It was the African controlled Beginning Passage—the land route that ran from Africa's interior to the coast—where most African slaves died, mainly from abuse, disease, exposure, neglect, animal depredations, and outright murder.

This was due not just to the shock of capture, but also to exhaustion, hyperthermia, malnourishment, sleep deprivation, dehydration, illness, animal attacks, and the inevitable physical abuse suffered at the hands of their tyrannical African captors. All of this made the misery and the mortality rates of the Middle Passage—which were after all, as one historian noted, merely part of "the then customary dangers and hardships of the sea"—pale in comparison.

Most importantly, let us note here that the Middle Passage was operated by European and American whites, while the Beginning Passage, part of the domestic African slavery system, was run and controlled strictly by Africans.[64]

FACT 48

YANKEE SLAVE SHIPS WERE SAILING TO AFRICA RIGHT INTO THE CIVIL WAR PERIOD

As proof we have the example of Captain Nathaniel Gordon of New York, the only American ever tried, convicted, and executed for slaving. His death occurred on February 21, 1862, at President Lincoln's personal order.

The infamous slave ship, U.S.S. Nightingale of New York, with the U.S. flag waving from her stern.

More evidence comes from the *Nightingale*, the last American slave ship to be captured by the U.S. government. The New York slaver was confiscated on April 21, 1861. Known fondly to Northerners as the "Prince of Slavers," the *Nightingale* was built in Maine, fitted out in New Hampshire, sailed from Massachusetts, and had a New York captain.

At the time of her seizure, this vessel, from the so-called "abolitionist North," had nearly 1,000 manacled Africans on board. She was doing "business as usual" up until the first few weeks of the Civil War, all the while proudly flying the U.S. flag from her mast.[65]

The execution of Yankee slaver Captain Nathaniel Gordon (of Maine) in New York City, February 21, 1862.

FACT 49

ABRAHAM LINCOLN WAS NOT THE "FRIEND OF BLACKS" OR THE "GREAT EMANCIPATOR"

According to not only his party members but his own words, U.S. President Abraham Lincoln stalled emancipation, blocked black civil rights, promoted American apartheid, and spent his entire adult life pushing for the deportation of blacks. Furthermore, he was a lifelong supporter and onetime leader of the racist Yankee organization, the American Colonization Society, whose stated goal was to make America "white from coast to coast," by shipping out as many blacks as possible to foreign lands.

In point of fact, Lincoln was a callous Leftist and a publicly avowed white racist, white supremacist, and white separatist whose plans for African-Americans included corralling them in their own all-black state and exiling the rest back "to their own native land," as he phrased it in a speech at Peoria, Illinois, on October 16, 1854.

Not only that, Lincoln's Emancipation Proclamation did not actually free a single slave. This was because his edict only liberated slaves in the Confederate States, a sovereign nation where he had no legal authority, while leaving slavery intact in the United States, where he had full legal authority. For these reasons alone—and there are many others—Lincoln cannot be considered either the "friend of the black man" or the "Great Emancipator."[66]

LINCOLN
and the
COMMUNISTS
By Earl Browder

The cover of Earl Browder's suppressed book *Lincoln and the Communists*. What pro-North writers will not tell you is that Republican President Abe Lincoln was actually a socialistic white racist, supremacist, and separatist (who is still adored by progressives, racial bigots, communists, and dictators); one who did more to damage, block, and delay black civil rights than anyone else in the 19th-Century. African-Americans, in fact, had no chance of *true* and *lasting* freedom as long as Lincoln was alive—which is why the Thirteenth Amendment came only after his death.

FACT 50

JEFFERSON DAVIS WAS BOTH THE REAL FRIEND OF BLACKS & THE TRUE GREAT EMANCIPATOR

While Lincoln was plotting the exile of all blacks from America's shores, Confederate President Jefferson Davis and his wife Varina (Howell) adopted a young black boy, Jim Limber, who they raised as their own in the Confederate White House. During the War they always treated their black servants equitably and with the greatest respect, as part of their family in fact. And after Lee's surrender, during the Davis family's escape southward, their coachman was a "faithful" free black.

Anti-South historians do not want you to know that Confederate President Jefferson Davis planned on full abolition in the South almost a year before the ratification of the Thirteenth Amendment, making him America's true Great Emancipator.

Later, after the War, the one-time Rebel president and his wife sold their plantation, Brierfield, to a former slave. Davis even spoke once of a time when he led "negroes against a lawless body of armed white men . . .," something we can be sure that white separatist Lincoln never did—or would have even considered.

Finally, Davis was against black colonization (preferring that blacks remain in the South, where they had been since the 1500s), banned the foreign slave trade in the Confederacy four years before the Union did, and committed the C.S. to complete abolition in January 1865, almost a year before the U.S. implemented the Thirteenth Amendment. For these reasons alone Davis must be considered not only the real friend of blacks, but the true Great Emancipator.[67]

FACT 51

IT WAS THE NORTH'S DEPENDENCE ON THE YANKEE SLAVE TRADE, NOT SOUTHERN SLAVERY, THAT LAUNCHED THE CIVIL WAR

We have long been taught that the North fought the Confederacy over Southern slavery. Again, the opposite is true. It was the North's heavy dependence on the Yankee slave trade and on selling its slaves to the South, that helped precipitate the Civil War.

This 19th-Century photo—entitled "King Cotton and his Slaves"—of a group of black Mississippi servants transporting bales of cotton, reveals the real motivation behind Lincoln's hatred of Southern secession: the lucrative American slave industry. When the Southern states began to secede, Northern industrialists and Yankee slave ship owners feared that they would lose control of their most valuable revenue streams: sales of African slaves to the South and the purchase of slave-produced cotton from the South. This is precisely how and why Lincoln got elected, as his Inaugural Speech on March 4, 1861, proves: in the address he promised not to interfere with either the Yankee slave trade or Southern slavery.

In March 1861 the newly constitutionally formed Confederate States of America adopted its Constitution, which included a clause banning slave trading with foreign nations. "Foreign nations," of course, now included the United States of America. The North panicked, deciding it was better to beat the South into submission than allow her to cut off one of her primary revenue streams: the transatlantic Yankee slave trade.

Big government Liberal Abraham Lincoln, the only 1860 presidential candidate who promised *not* to interfere with slavery, and who was put into office by Northern industrialists using profits from the Northern slave trade, launched the War of Northern Aggression in April, just a few weeks later.[68]

FACT 52

CONFEDERATE PRESIDENT JEFFERSON DAVIS SAID THAT THE WAR WAS NOT OVER SLAVERY

It is patently clear to all rational thinking individuals that slavery itself had nothing to do with the Civil War. For one thing, if slavery had been the "cause," the War would have ended on September 22, 1862, when Lincoln issued his Preliminary Emancipation Proclamation, or at least by January 1, 1863, when he issued his Final Emancipation Proclamation. Yet, the bloody, illegal, and unnecessary conflict continued for another two years.

The Confederacy's highest leader, President Davis, held that slavery was not the direct cause of the Civil War.

Furthermore, it would have cost ten times less to simply free America's slaves than to go to war. Not even the megalomaniacal Lincoln, with all of his psychological problems and emotional disabilities, was mentally unbalanced enough to overlook this important fact.

However, the most damning evidence against the Yankee myth that "slavery triggered the Civil War" comes from the top political and military leaders of both the Confederacy and the Union. Here is how C.S. President Jefferson Davis put it:

> The truth remains intact and incontrovertible, that *the existence of African servitude was in no wise the cause of the conflict*, but only an incident. In the later controversies that arose, however, its effect in operating as a lever upon the passions, prejudices, or sympathies of mankind, was so potent that it has been spread like a thick cloud over the whole horizon of historic truth.[69]

FACT 53

CONFEDERATE VICE PRESIDENT ALEXANDER H. STEPHENS SAID THAT THE WAR WAS NOT OVER SLAVERY

To the last day of his life our celebrated vice president, Alexander H. Stephens, declared that the South seceded for one reason and one reason only: to "render our liberties and institutions more secure" by "rescuing, restoring, and re-establishing the Constitution."

As for the War, the South took up arms, he often noted, for no other reason than a "desire to preserve constitutional liberty and perpetuate the government in its purity."[70]

The Confederacy's second highest leader, Vice President Alexander H. Stephens, maintained that slavery had no connection to the War.

FACT 54

Confederate General Robert E. Lee Said that the War was Not Over Slavery

According to one of the South's most admired generals, Robert E. Lee:

> All the South has ever desired was that the Union as established by our forefathers should be preserved; and that the government as originally organized should be administered in purity and truth.[71]

General Robert E. Lee, the Confederacy's highest ranking military officer, tacitly proclaimed that slavery was not the reason the South went to war.

FACT 55

UNION PRESIDENT ABRAHAM LINCOLN SAID THAT THE WAR WAS NOT OVER SLAVERY

No one was more definitive about the true purpose, and thus the cause, of the "Civil War" than the man who started it: U.S. President Abraham Lincoln. In his Inaugural Address, March 4, 1861, only four weeks before the conflict, he declared: "I have no purpose, directly or indirectly, to interfere with the institution of slavery in the States where it exists." In the Summer of 1861, with the War now in full swing, he told Reverend Charles E. Lester:

> I think [Massachusetts Senator Charles] Sumner, and the rest of you [abolitionists], would upset our apple-cart altogether, if you had your way. . . . We didn't go into the war to put down Slavery, but to put the flag back . . .

The Union's highest leader, President Abraham Lincoln, repeatedly stated that the abolition of slavery was not the purpose of the War.

On August 22, 1862, he sent this public comment to Horace Greeley, owner of the New York *Tribune*:

> My paramount object in this struggle is to save the Union, and it is not either to save or destroy slavery. If I could save the Union without freeing any slave, I would do it . . .

Impatient over misunderstandings on the topic, on August 15, 1864, he clarified his position yet again:

> My enemies pretend I am now carrying on this war for the sole purpose of abolition. So long as I am President, it shall be carried on for the sole purpose of restoring the Union.[72]

FACT 56

THE U.S. CONGRESS SAID THAT THE WAR WAS NOT OVER SLAVERY

The U.S. Congress also testified that the Civil War had no connection to slavery. On July 22, 1861, it issued the following resolution:

> . . . this war is not waged upon our part in any spirit of oppression, nor for any purpose of conquest or subjugation, *nor purpose of overthrowing or interfering with the rights or established institutions [that is, slavery] of those States*; but to defend and maintain the supremacy of the Constitution and to preserve the Union with all the dignity, equality, and rights of the several States unimpaired; that *as soon as these objects are accomplished the war ought to cease.*[73]

On July 22, 1861, the U.S. Congress published a resolution announcing the reason the U.S. waged war on the Confederacy. It was not for the "purpose of overthrowing or interfering with the rights or established institutions" of the Southern states, the document clearly asserted, but to "preserve the Union."

FACT 57

UNION GENERAL ULYSSES S. GRANT SAID THAT THE WAR WAS NOT OVER SLAVERY

The North's most famous general, Ulysses S. Grant, made this comment on the topic of slavery and the cause of the War:

> The sole object of this war is to restore the union. Should I be convinced it has any other object, or that the government designs using its soldiers to execute the wishes of the Abolitionists, I pledge to you my honor as a man and a soldier, I would resign my commission and carry my sword to the other side.[74]

General Ulysses S. Grant, the Union's highest ranking military officer, avowed that slavery was not the reason the North invaded the South.

FACT 58

IN REALITY LINCOLN WAGED WAR ON THE SOUTHERN CONFEDERACY IN ORDER TO INSTALL BIG GOVERNMENT AT WASHINGTON

Why was the War fought then, if not over slavery? Lincoln claimed it was to "preserve the union." But this was just a smokescreen to conceal his true Liberal agenda: to install big government, then known as the "American System," in Washington.

Devised and promoted by Lincoln's political hero, slave owner Henry Clay—a man "Honest Abe" called "my *beau ideal* of a statesman, the man for whom I fought all my humble life"—the American System was a nationalist program in which there was to be a single sovereign authority, the president, who was to assume the role of a kinglike ruler with autocratic powers.

Likewise, the government at Washington, D.C. was to be federated, acting as a consolidated superpower that would eventually control the money supply, offer internal improvements, intervene in foreign affairs, nationalize the banking system, issue soaring tariffs, grant subsidies to corporations, engage in protectionism, and impose an income tax, all hints of Lincoln's coming empire.

In essence, what the American System proposed was a federated government that was the polar opposite of a confederated government. Under federation, its proponents, the Federalists, Monarchists, or Hamiltonians (named after Liberal Alexander Hamilton), as they were variously called, not only sought to create a large, domineering, all-powerful, nationalized government to which all interests (from private to business) were subordinate, but they also proposed that the states be largely stripped of their independence and authority, then placed in an inferior role. Hamilton himself wanted to get rid of the states altogether. Jeffersonianism was to be abolished and replaced with the

Hamiltonian or American System.[75]

As such, nation-building nationalist Lincoln must be considered nothing less than the "Great Federator": the creator of American big government for big business, with its big spending, Big Brother mindset. He is also either fully or partially responsible for the following: America's internal revenue program (the IRS), American protectionism, American imperialism, American expansionism, America's bloated military despotism, America's enormous standing army, America's central banking system, America's corporate welfare system (which Lincoln called "internal improvements"), America's nation-building agenda, and America's deeply entangled foreign alliances. (Lincoln apparently never read Jefferson's admonition that America's approach to foreign affairs should be: "Peace, commerce, and honest friendship with all nations, entangling alliances with none.")

Thanks to Lincoln's authoritarian policies, his trampling of the U.S. Constitution, his attempt to destroy states' rights, and his dictatorial efforts to install big government at Washington, D.C., he won the admiration of socialists around the world, most notably arch socialist and German Nazi leader Adolf Hitler.

Is it any wonder that anti-Confederacy Lincoln surrounded himself with Marxists, that he was supported by a group of radical socialists called the "Forty-Eighters," or that he was adored by nationalists, dictators, and communists from around the world, including socialists like Adolf Hitler and Francis Bellamy (author of America's *Pledge of Allegiance*)?[76]

And here, politically at least, is Lincoln's greatest legacy, for big government opened the door to federal tyranny and its many dangers and horrors: the consolidation of governmental powers, the centralization of executive power, unchecked presidential power, the growth of the nanny state, unlimited abuses and corruption, and the progressive, intrusive, oppressive, tax-and-spend government that American citizens now labor under, whether they are Lincolnian Liberals themselves, or Independent, Conservative, or Libertarian. And all of this came at the expense of individual civil liberties and states' rights, the very rights our colonial and Confederate ancestors fought and died for.[77]

FACT 59

IN 1862 LINCOLN ISSUED A HUMAN "BLOCKADE" TO PREVENT FREED SOUTHERN BLACK SLAVES FROM MIGRATING INTO THE NORTHERN STATES

It was the same Yankee bigotry possessed by Lincoln that prompted one of his loyal employees, David Davis, associate justice of the Supreme Court, to go to the president and complain that an "excess" of freed Southern slaves venturing into Illinois would jeopardize the upcoming 1864 election. Lincoln agreed, issuing what John Y. Simon referred to as a human "blockade," one meant to halt even the possibility of a "negro influx" northward.

From then on Southern blacks made refugees by Lincoln's War were restricted to camps set up in the South by Union officers, where they were forced to work cotton under armed guard. Few white Northerners, especially Lincoln, wanted to be "tied down and helpless, and run over like sheep," as he himself put it, by an advancing horde of Southern African-Americans.[78]

When associate justice of the Supreme Court, David Davis, complained to Lincoln that freed blacks coming north would hurt his chances at the polls in the upcoming 1864 presidential election, the racist chief executive immediately issued a human "blockade" to prevent being "run over like sheep" by a great "negro influx." Lincoln and his bigoted cronies need not have worried, however. Most Southern blacks had no interest in moving to or even visiting the racially intolerant Northern states.

FACT 60

THE CONFEDERACY ENLISTED BLACK
SOLDIERS LONG BEFORE THE UNION DID

The South's first all-black militia was officially formed on April 23, 1861, only nine days after the first battle of the War at Fort Sumter, South Carolina. The unit, known as the "Native Guards (colored)," was "duly and legally enrolled as a part of the militia of the State, its officers being commissioned by Thomas O. Moore, Governor and Commander-in-Chief of the State of Louisiana . . ."

Black Confederate soldiers from Louisiana's Native Guards protecting a Southern railroad.

In contrast, the North's first all-black militia, the First South Carolina Volunteers, was not commissioned until over a year and a half later (on November 7, 1862), under Yankee Colonel Thomas Wentworth Higginson.

Indeed, Lincoln did not allow *official* black enlistment until January 1, 1863, with the issuance of his Final Emancipation Proclamation, as that document tacitly states. Up until then he had strictly barred both blacks and Native-Americans (whom his administration referred to as "savages") from joining the Union military as armed soldiers.

Since blacks had served officially, legally, and courageously as soldiers in *all* of America's conflicts up until the Civil War, Lincoln must be named as the one who injected white racism and racial segregation into the U.S. military for the first time, an unfortunate situation that lasted well into the late 1940s.[79]

FACT 61

THE NORTHERN ARMIES WERE RACIALLY SEGREGATED, THE SOUTHERN ARMIES WERE RACIALLY INTEGRATED

Lincoln, a dyed-in-the-wool white separatist, was literally obsessed with the idea of American apartheid (the geographical segregation of the races), which is one reason why, when he was a member of the Illinois legislature, he asked for funds to expel all free blacks from the state. This was also the reason he became a manager of the Illinois chapter of the American Colonization Society, which one day hoped to make the entire U.S. "as white as New England."

As this 19th-Century illustration correctly depicts, Confederate white and black soldiers served in the same units and fought side by side as equals, quite unlike in the Union's segregated armies.

Not surprisingly, after finally allowing official black enlistment in 1863, Lincoln ordered all of his black troops to be racially segregated, led by white officers, and paid half that of white enlistees, infuriating both his black soldiery and Northern abolitionists.

Naturally, in the far more racially tolerant South, birthplace of the American abolition movement, President Davis simply integrated blacks directly into his army and navy. As in Southern society itself, there was no desire for segregation among the South's military forces. For unlike in the racist North, Southern troops neither wanted segregation or needed it.[80]

FACT 62

AS MANY AS 1 MILLION AFRICAN-AMERICANS FOUGHT FOR THE CONFEDERACY

The truth that you will never read in pro-North Civil War histories is that far more blacks fought for the Confederacy than for the Union. The Union possessed about 3 million soldiers. Of these about 200,000 were black, 6 percent of the total. The Confederacy had about 1 million soldiers. Of these an estimated 300,000 were black, 30 percent of the total. Simply put: 30 percent of Davis' army was black, but only 6 percent of Lincoln's army was black.

And these numbers are conservative if we use the definition of a "private soldier" as determined by German-American Union General August Valentine Kautz in 1864:

> In the fullest sense, *any man in the military service who receives pay, whether sworn in or not, is a soldier*, because he is subject to military law. Under this general head, laborers, teamsters, sutlers, chaplains, etc., are soldiers.[81]

By Kautz's definition of a "private soldier," some 2 million Southerners fought for the Confederacy: 1 million whites and perhaps as many as 1 million blacks. As most of the 4 million blacks (3.5 million servants, 500,000 free) living in the South at the time of Lincoln's War remained loyal to the Confederacy, and as at least 1 million of these either worked in or fought in the Rebel army and navy in some capacity, Kautz' definition raises the percentage of Southern blacks who defended the Confederacy as real soldiers to as much as 50 percent of the total Confederate soldier population—five times or 500 percent more than fought for the Union.[82]

FACT 63

THE NORTHERN STATES NEVER ACTUALLY OFFICIALLY ABOLISHED SLAVERY

nti-South writers tell us that the Northern states "abolished slavery completely by the early 1800s," but this is simply not true. Indeed, the North never really abolished slavery at all. This term, pertaining to Yankee slavery, is, in truth, a misnomer. What the Northern states actually did was merely suppress the institution until, over time, it naturally faded away due to neglect, unprofitability, and ultimately white racist hostility. This was accomplished through a slow and voluntarily process; one, it should be emphasized, that took place *without any interference from the South*.

This exposes the lie that the Northern states literally "abolished slavery" within their borders on a precise date in a specific year, as our Yankee-biased history books claim. For example: "Vermont in 1777," "Pennsylvania in 1780," "Massachusetts in 1780," "Connecticut in 1784," "Rhode Island in 1784," "New Jersey in 1804," and "New York in 1827."

The fact of the matter is that *none* of the Northern states ever legally ended the institution; they only legislated it into "gradual extinction." This is why a few Yankee states, such as New Hampshire and Delaware, did not fully rid themselves of slavery until the passage of the Thirteenth Amendment, December 6, 1865 (note that the U.S. government continued to allow the enslavement of criminals).

In short, while Pennsylvania, Connecticut, Rhode Island, and New Hampshire all intentionally used a *gradual emancipation plan* (wherein freedom was guaranteed to all persons born in their states after the date of so-called "abolition"), the North as a whole gave herself over 200 leisurely years to eliminate slavery from within her borders. This is hardly what one would describe as "quick and complete abolition," as pro-North historians refer to it.[83]

FACT 64

THE NORTH REFUSED TO GRANT THE SOUTH THE SAME AMOUNT OF TIME TO ABOLISH SLAVERY IN ITS OWN REGION

Thanks to meddlesome Yankee, anti-slavery advocate William Lloyd Garrison of Massachusetts, from 1831 on Northern abolitionists began demanding immediate, complete, and uncompensated emancipation across the South—this coming from the very section of the country that gave birth to both the American slave trade and American slavery!

No one likes to be ordered around, including Southerners; especially not by self-righteous, liberal do-gooders such as Garrison, who have no respect for the rights, ways, and mannerisms of other people, but only simply want to impose their views on those who do not agree with them.

Though the South had been the center of American abolitionism for a half century by this time, she understood that one could not rush the operation. *Complete* abolition was a complex procedure that had taken other countries years, decades, centuries, to complete, and it would take Dixie just as long, or longer. Time was needed to prepare, from designing laws and rules to regulate the process of readying 3.5 million former slaves for a life of freedom, to finding the capital ($3 billion, or $57 billion in today's currency) to compensate former slave owners and establish housing and jobs for freedmen and women.

Dixie only asked the North for the same amount of time to develop a functional emancipation program that it had given itself. But this the North would not do. The slavery issue came to be used as a Yankee sledge hammer to force Northern ideas on the South. The South resisted, claiming states' rights under the U.S. Constitution. The North ignored her, and as Lincoln disingenuously said, "the war came."[84]

FACT 65

THE NORTH DID NOT ABOLISH
SLAVERY FOR HUMANITARIAN REASONS

Although there were a myriad of reasons why slavery was gradually and officially extinguished in the Northern states, not one of them had to do with humanitarian or civil rights concerns about slaves themselves. The worldly Victorian Yankee felt no apprehension, shame, or guilt for engaging in the "sin" of slavery. Thus when it came time to destroy it he was motivated by reasons of an entirely practical nature, all which can be pared down to three primary factors.

The "tail" side of an American Colonization Society one cent token, issued in 1833 for newly deported American blacks living in the organization's most important colony, Liberia. The development of Liberia delighted President Lincoln, who was himself not only a devoted benefactor of the colony, but was at one time an ACS official in Illinois. His ongoing efforts in the cause of black deportation prompted one of his party's liberal members, Massachusetts-born Samuel Clarke Pomeroy, to suggest naming a freedmen's colony in Latin America, "Linconia."

The first reason the North wanted to rid itself of slavery was that it eventually became unprofitable (the same reason Europe finally abolished it). And slavery became unprofitable in the American North, in great part, due to the regions's largely rocky sandy soil, hilly terrain, and short cool summers, all which made it unsuitable for large-scale farming.

Second, there was the North's enormous distance from both

Africa (where slaves were picked up) and the tropics (where slaves were needed on sugar, coffee, cotton, pineapple, tobacco, and indigo plantations). This made it much more profitable to sell slaves in the American South (which was a shorter distance from both Africa and the Caribbean) than transport them back up to, for example, Rhode Island.

Third, along with the North's growing blue-collar demographic (which made Northern slavery more and more redundant) came increasing racial intolerance toward non-whites. As early as the late 1700s white Northerners "were frankly stating an antipathy of their people toward negroes in any capacity whatever." This, of course, now made abolition in the North absolutely essential, especially economically. Yankee John Adams of Massachusetts, who was to become America's second president two years later, wrote the following in a personal letter dated March 21, 1795:

> Argument might have some weight in the abolition of slavery in the Massachusetts, but the real cause was the multiplication of labouring white people, who would no longer suffer the rich to employ these sable rivals so much to their injury. This principle has kept negro slavery out of France, England, and other parts of Europe. The common people would not suffer the labour, by which alone they could obtain a subsistence, to be done by slaves. . . . The common white people, or rather the labouring people, were the cause of rendering negroes unprofitable servants. *Their scoffs and insults, their continual insinuations, filled the negroes with discontent, made them lazy, idle, proud, vicious, and at length wholly useless to their masters, to such a degree that the abolition of slavery became a measure of economy.*[85]

Here we have the most significant factor leading to the death of Northern slavery: *Northern white racism.* Most 18th- and 19th-Century Yanks simply preferred living in an all-white society, free from the "naturally disgusting" presence of the black man, as Lincoln and other white racist Northerners expressed it. It was this very sentiment which gave birth to the bigoted American Colonization Society, a popular Yankee black deportation organization founded in 1816 in Washington, D.C., by a Northerner, New Jerseyan Robert Finley—and supported by Lincoln, Harriet Beecher Stowe, Horace Greeley, Garrison, Jared Sparks, Henry Rutgers, and Edward Everett, as well as many other Yanks of note.[86]

FACT 66

THE SOUTH WAS WORKING ON PLANS TO END SLAVERY WHEN LINCOLN ILLEGALLY & UNNECESSARILY INVADED DIXIE

Beginning in the 1600s we have numerous records of Southerners seeking the abolition of both the slave trade and slavery. Indeed, the American abolition movement got its start in the South, in Virginia, to be exact, where, in 1655, the first voluntary emancipation in the American colonies took place.[87] In the 1700s some of the more famous of the Virginia abolitionists were George Washington, Thomas Jefferson, James Madison, and George Mason.

By the early 1800s the American abolition movement was at its peak across Dixie. Of the 130 abolition societies established before 1827 by Northern abolitionist Benjamin Lundy, over 100, comprising four-fifths of the total membership, were in the South. Southern Quakers were among the first to come out against the spread of the institution. Early North Carolina, as another example, had a number of well-known "forceful" antislavery leaders, such as Benjamin Sherwood Hedrick and Daniel Reaves Goodlow. And in South Carolina the famed Quaker sisters Sarah and Angelina Grimké were just two among millions of Southerners fighting for the cause of abolition. The Southern abolition movement involved so many Southerners, so many Southern states, and covered such a large span of time, that the latter Grimké sister wrote an entire book on the subject.

As noted, other esteemed Southerners who came out against the "peculiar institution" were James G. Birney, Dyer Burgess, James A. Thome, Samuel Doak, William Ladd, James Lemen, Gideon Blackburn, James Gilliland, David Nelson, James H. Dickey, Samuel Crothers, Bishop William Meade, John Rankin, Nathaniel Macon, Edward Coles, William T. Allan, Christopher Gadsden, and George Bourne, cofounder of the "American Anti-Slavery Society" in 1833. On August 14, 1776, South Carolina rice planter and slave owner Henry Laurens wrote the following to his son John, who was also antislavery:

> You know, my dear son, *I abhor slavery. I was born in a country in which slavery had been established by British Parliaments and the laws of the country for ages before my existence.* I found the Christian religion and slavery growing under the same authority and cultivation. I nevertheless dislike it. In former days there was no combating the prejudices of men, supported by interest [money]. The day I hope is approaching when from principles of gratitude and justice every man will strive to be foremost in complying with the golden rule. £20,000 sterling [about £2.5 million, or $4 million in today's currency] would my negroes produce if sold at auction tomorrow. *I am not the man who enslaved them; they are indebted to Englishmen for that favour. Nevertheless I am devising means for manumitting many of them and for cutting off the entail of slavery.*[88]

What our Yankee biased history books do not teach is that from the 1600s on, every year thousands of Southerners simply emancipated their slaves, all without any prompting from the North. Among them were slave owners like Nathan Bedford Forrest, who freed his slaves even before Lincoln's War in 1861, and Robert E. Lee, who liberated his wife's servants before the Emancipation Proclamation was issued in 1863. Unlike in the North, there were no laws against manumission in Dixie, so Southerners gave full vent to their humanitarian instincts.

Thomas Jefferson had been working on Southern abolition from his first days as an American statesmen, and was responsible for prohibiting the American slave trade after the year 1808 (tragically, Yankee slave traders ignored the ban, continuing to sail to Africa right into the Civil War period). Indeed, it was Jefferson's criticism of Britain for imposing slavery on the 13 original American colonies that helped instigate the American Revolution,[89] which in turn led directly to the first "Confederate States of America"—as the U.S.A. was known in the 1700s and 1800s.[90]

The South was still struggling with precisely how to initiate full abolition, or what Jefferson aptly compared to holding "a wolf behind the ears," when Lincoln tricked the South into firing the first shot of his war at the Battle of Fort Sumter on April 12, 1861.[91]

FACT 67

THE AMERICAN SOUTH WAS THE LAST REGION IN THE WEST TO PRACTICE SLAVERY & THE FIRST TO TRY TO ABOLISH IT

In 1749 Georgia became the last of the 13 British-American colonies to legalize slavery. This was long after every Western nation had already adopted the institution. Seventeen years earlier, in 1732, Georgia became the first colony to place a prohibition against commercial trafficking in slaves into her state constitution, making the American South the first Western region to move toward abolition.

Around the same time, dozens of abolition societies began to spring up across Dixie, with Virginia leading the way in white America's tireless attempt to end slavery—which began in the Dominion State with, as noted, the first voluntary emancipation in 1655.[92]

Virginian and U.S. President Thomas Jefferson, one of America's earliest and most determined abolitionists.

FACT 68

ACCORDING TO COUNTLESS EYEWITNESSES THE OLD NORTH WAS FAR MORE RACIST THAN THE OLD SOUTH

S cores of eyewitness accounts, both domestic and foreign, reveal that the Old North was far more racist than the Old South. As early as 1831 individuals like French aristocrat Alexis de Tocqueville, who toured the South and the North that year, noticed that Southerners were "much more tolerant and compassionate" toward blacks than Northerners. This is why, while visiting America in the 1850s, Englishman Sir Charles Lyell observed that the Southern states justifiably "make louder professions than the Northerners of democratic principles and love of equality."

The racial discrepancy between the South and the North was also remarked on by British journalists, even in the middle of the Civil War. In 1862 the *North British Review* noted that in the North, "where slavers are fitted out by scores . . . free Negroes are treated like lepers." This was the same year Union President Abraham Lincoln issued his Preliminary Emancipation Proclamation, which, of course, called for continued efforts to deport all freed blacks out of the U.S.

Alexis de Tocqueville

After his travels across the U.S. in 1831 and 1832, Tocqueville summed up his observations this way:

> Whosoever has inhabited the United States must have perceived that in those parts of the Union in which the negroes are no longer slaves, they have in no wise drawn nearer to the whites. On the contrary, *the prejudice of the race appears to be stronger in the States which have abolished slavery than in those where it still exists; and nowhere is it so intolerant as in those States where servitude never has been known.* [93]

FACT 69

THERE WERE TENS OF THOUSANDS OF BOTH AFRICAN-AMERICAN & NATIVE-AMERICAN SLAVE OWNERS

Liberal historians carefully hide the fact from the general public, but the reality is that there were tens of thousands of black slave owners in early America, most who were not counted in the U.S. Census (Census takers were prone to vastly underreporting blacks, free and enslaved). Additionally, some black slaveholders abused and whipped their African servants, another fact that you will seldom find in pro-North, anti-South history books.

In 1830 some 3,700 free Southern blacks owned nearly 12,000 black slaves, an average of almost four slaves a piece. That same year in the Deep South alone nearly 8,000 slaves were owned by some 1,500 black slave owners (about five slaves apiece). In Charleston, South Carolina, as another example, between the years 1820 and 1840, 75 percent of the city's free blacks owned slaves. Furthermore, *25 percent of all free American blacks owned slaves, South and North.*

It is important to remember that in 1861 the South's 300,000 white slave owners made up only 1 percent of the total U.S. white population of 30 million people. Thus, while only one Southern white out of every 300,000 owned slaves (1 percent), one Southern black out of every four owned slaves (25 percent). In other words, far more Southern blacks owned black (and sometimes white) slaves than Southern whites did: 25 percent compared to 1 percent.

Most Southern black slave owners were not only proslavery, they were also pro-South, supporting the Confederate Cause during Lincoln's War as fervently as any white Southerner did. At church each Sunday thousands of blacks would pray for those blacks, both their own slaves and their free friends, who wore the Rebel uniform. Their supplications were simple: they asked God to help all African-American Confederates kill as many Yankees as possible, then return home safely.

Wealthy blacks bought, sold, and exploited black slaves for profit, just as white slave owners did. The well-known Anna Kingsley, who began life—as was nearly always the case—as a slave in her native Africa, ended up in what is now Jacksonville, Florida, where she became one of early America's many black plantation owners and slaveholders.

Some, like the African-American Metoyers, an anti-abolition family from Louisiana, owned huge numbers of black slaves; in their case, at least 400. At about $1,500 a piece, their servants were worth a total of $600,000, or $20 million in today's currency. This made the Metoyers among the wealthiest people in the U.S., black or white, then or now. Louisiana's all-black Confederate army unit, the Augustin Guards, was named after the family patriarch, Augustin Metoyer.

Native-Americans with a newly captured white slave woman.

Black slavery was not just common among blacks. It was also found among America's 19th-Century Indians, who bought and sold African chattel right alongside black and white slave owners. In fact, one of the many reasons so many Native-Americans sided with the Southern Confederacy was that she promised to enforce the fugitive slave law in Indian Territory, making it a legal requirement to return runaway slaves to their original Indian owners.

While the average white slave owner owned five or less slaves (often only one or two), the average red slaveholder owned six. One Choctaw slaver owned 227. Again, it was *non-white* slave owners who individually owned the most slaves, not whites.

Slavery was practiced right up until the 1950s by some Native-American tribes, principally the Haida and the Tlingit peoples of the Pacific Northwest. Among the Haida, slaves performed all of the menial labor, ate only food scraps, were refused health care, and could not own property. And since there were no laws of protection, Haida slaves could be purchased, sold, beaten, molested, and even murdered at the whim of their owners. This is *true* slavery, the exact opposite of the much milder servitude experienced by Africans in the Old American South. [94]

FACT 70

LINCOLN WAS NOT AGAINST SLAVERY, ONLY THE SPREAD OF SLAVERY

Lincoln always did what was most politically expedient at the moment, a trait for which he was roundly criticized, even by members of his own party and constituency. However, there was one topic on which he never wavered: slavery. But contrary to Yankee myth, Lincoln's number one goal when it came to slavery was never to totally eliminate it. It was merely to *limit* its growth, as he himself said on numerous occasions. He only later acquiesced to the idea of *complete* abolition due to pressure from party radicals and political self-interest.

On December 22, 1860, in a letter to Southerner and soon-to-be Confederate Vice President Alexander H. Stephens, Lincoln wrote: "You think slavery . . . ought to be extended; while we think it . . . ought to be restricted." "Honest Abe," for once being completely honest, ended his letter to Stephens with this sensational statement: This is the "only substantial difference between us."

Just a few months later, on March 4, 1861, he would repeat the same sentiment almost word for word in his First Inaugural Address:

> One section of our country believes slavery . . . ought to be extended, while the other believes it . . . ought not . . . be extended. This is the only substantial dispute.[95]

Thus, just prior to the War, Lincoln held that the only real difference between the South's view of slavery and the North's was that the former wanted to allow it to spread (mainly into the new Western Territories, eventually to become America's Western states), while the latter wanted to contain it where it already existed (that is, mainly in the South). No mention of emancipation or abolition. Just limitation.

Six years earlier, in his debate with Stephen A. Douglas on October 16, 1854, at Peoria, Illinois, Lincoln outlined his reasons for wanting to restrict, not end, slavery:

> Whether slavery shall go into Nebraska, or other new Territories, is not a matter of exclusive concern to the people who may go there. The whole nation is interested that the best use shall be made of these Territories. *We want them for homes of free white people. This they cannot be, to any considerable extent, if slavery shall be planted within them. Slave States are places for poor white people to remove from, not to remove to. New free States are the places for poor people to go to, and better their condition. For this use the nation needs these Territories.*[96]

Four years later, on October 15, 1858, at Alton, Illinois, in his seventh and final joint debate with Douglas, Lincoln reasserted his views on the matter, this time even more vigorously:

> Now, irrespective of the moral aspect of this question as to whether there is a right or wrong in enslaving a negro, *I am still in favor of our new Territories being in such a condition that white men may find a home—may find some spot where they can better their condition—where they can settle upon new soil, and better their condition in life. I am in favor of this not merely (I must say it here as I have elsewhere) for our own people [that is, whites] who are born amongst us, but as an outlet for free white people everywhere, the world over—in which Hans, and Baptiste, and Patrick, and all other men from all the world, may find new homes and better their condition in life.*[97]

As he declared in a speech on June 26, 1857, the deportation of blacks was the only way to prevent whites from having to live in close association with them. But,

> as an *immediate* separation is impossible the next best thing is to *keep them apart where they are not already together.*[98]

Thus, even if his racist colonization plan did not work out, he knew of other ways of "keeping whites and blacks apart where they are not already together."

Limiting the spread of slavery into the North was important to Lincoln and other Yankee racists for a number of reasons, though there was one that stood out above all the others. By forcing slavery to stay in the South they believed that this would also serve as an ideal method of "race control": keeping blacks in bondage in Dixie meant that Northerners need not worry about a "flood of darkies" coming over the Mason-Dixon Line any time soon, with whites "tied down and helpless, and run over like sheep," as Lincoln bluntly put it. With slavery confined to the South, Yanks could continue to promote antislavery views without fear of having to actually deal with the "unthinkable horror" of how to handle 3.5 million newly freed, hungry, homeless, and jobless blacks, many of them illiterate, armed, confused, and angry.

This is why for Lincoln the issue was never about permanent and total emancipation. Rather it was about containing the spread of slavery so that bigoted whites like himself would not have to intermingle with blacks. "If we do not let them [blacks] get together in the [Western] Territories," he said publicly on July 10, 1858, "they won't mix [with whites] there."

As U.S. President Woodrow Wilson writes, in Lincoln's mind it was not a question of slavery continuing in the South or anywhere else. It was a question of keeping it out of the newly developing Western

Liberal Senator Lyman Trumbull of Connecticut, like his boss President Lincoln, was not against slavery, but merely the spread of slavery outside the South. To emphasize their position, the Republicans (the Liberals of the day) began calling themselves "the white man's party."

Territories. On this issue in particular Lincoln had the "almost unanimous" support of the North, nearly all of whose inhabitants agreed with the president that the territories should remain "as white as New England." One of Lincoln's own senators, Lyman Trumbull, summed up the president's feelings on the matter perfectly when he referred to their political party as "the white man's party."[99]

FACT 71

FEW SLAVES ACTUALLY USED THE UNDERGROUND RAILROAD & IT WAS CONSIDERED A FAILURE BY MOST ABOLITIONISTS

The Underground Railroad was not the gargantuan, tightly organized, national antislavery system that pro-North writers claim it to have been. Though it functioned throughout most of the War, only about 2,000 slaves (just 500 servants a year) out of 4.5 million (North and South) availed themselves of it—a mere 0.04 percent of the total.

According to scholarly studies, few antebellum Southern slaves used the Railroad: the fugitive slaves that passed through New York, for instance, all came from Maryland and Delaware. Black Southern escapees preferred staying in Dixie, simply disappearing into the anonymity of the big Southern cities where they easily merged with the large free black population. (This is not surprising: even after Lincoln's Final Emancipation Proclamation was issued, 95 percent of all Southern slaves voluntarily stayed at home in Dixie.)

It is telling that the definitive early source on the "rail," William Still's 1872 book, *The Underground Railroad: A Record of Facts, Authentic Narratives, Letters, Etc.*, features not millions, not thousands, not even hundreds, but a mere handful of black slaves who were, as the author phrases it, "plucked from the jaws of slavery" via this particular method. And nearly all of these testimonials are of single individuals, with the exception of a few rare slave groups, usually comprising no more than four to six people.

In the end, as nearly all enslaved American blacks seeking freedom did so on their own and without any assistance, the so-called "Underground Railroad" was little more than a morale booster for abolitionists, as opposed to an actual effective escape system for slaves.[100]

FACT 72

THE CONFEDERATE STATES OF AMERICA WAS NOT A "SLAVE REGIME"

The Confederate States of America was not a "slave regime" or a "slavocracy," as anti-South partisans have maliciously and incorrectly labeled it. In 1860 only 4.8 percent of the total white male population of the South owned black servants, and this in the same region where the American abolition movement was born. This is hardly what could be called a "slave regime."

America did indeed have its slave regimes, but they were not in the South.

The first slavocracies existed among Native-Americans, who enslaved one another as a routine aspect of Indian society, using some of the most brutal and sadistic forms of slavery ever recorded. After European colonization, Native-Americans began enslaving untold thousands of whites, blacks, and browns as well.

After Britain imposed slavery on the original 13 American colonies, the Northern states happily continued practicing both the slave trade and slavery for 239 years, making the North, not the South, America's true slavocracy.

America's greatest slavocracy, however, emerged among the white colonists of the Northeast, where both the American slave trade and American slavery were born in the early 1600s. Of these states, New York came to be "America's Slave Capital," a true slave regime that imported and sold millions of (previously enslaved) Africans over a period of 239 years, far longer than any other state, North or South.[101]

FACT 73

THE SOUTHERN CONFEDERACY
NEVER ENGAGED IN THE SLAVE TRADE

As we have seen, the only American slave ships to ever sail from the U.S. left from Northern ports aboard Northern slave vessels, that were designed by Northern engineers, constructed by Northern shipbuilders, fitted out by Northern riggers, piloted by Northern ship captains, manned by Northern crews, launched from Northern marine ports, funded by Northern businessmen,

A slave sale at the slave port in Providence, Rhode Island.

all which was supported by the vast majority of the anti-abolitionist Northern population.

In other words, the American slave trade was a purely Yankee business, one that operated under the auspices of, not the Confederate Flag, but the U.S. Flag. Yet it is the Confederate Flag that is now associated with slavery. Such has been the overwhelming power of the North's revisionist version of American history that lies, slander, and disinformation concerning the Southern Confederacy have come to be regarded as fact![102]

FACT 74

THE SOUTHERN CONFEDERACY PLANNED TO END SLAVERY BEFORE THE U.S. DID

In January 1865 Confederate Secretary of State Judah P. Benjamin ordered Confederate commissioner Duncan F. Kenner to England to announce the C.S.'s commitment to full emancipation. This was nearly a year before the U.S. issued the Thirteenth Amendment (on December 6) banning slavery throughout the nation. (Let us note again that, contrary to Yankee mythology, the Northern states *never* officially abolished slavery. Instead they slowly and methodically destroyed the institution through a long drawn out process known as "gradual emancipation," taking over 100 years to complete the process, which finally ended in 1865 with the ratification of the Thirteenth Amendment. Tragically, the North refused to grant the South the same privilege, and instead demanded "immediate abolition," an impossibility at the time.)

The Confederacy's motion to abolish slavery across the South had the complete support of the Southern populace, of course, the very people who had inaugurated the American abolition movement in the early 1700s. One of the better known of the great Southern abolitionists was the celebrated antislavery Virginian, Robert E. Lee, who, on December 27, 1856—five years before Lincoln's War—made this comment about the "peculiar institution":

> There are few, I believe, in this enlightened age, but what will acknowledge that slavery as an institution is a moral and political evil in any country.

Later, during the War, like *all* Southern civilians and Confederate soldiers and officers, Lee supported the idea of immediate abolition and black enlistment, a fact you will never read in any pro-North book.[103]

FACT 75

THE CONFEDERATE MILITARY WAS MULTIRACIAL, MULTICULTURAL, & MULTIETHNIC

W e have been taught that the Confederate armies were "100 percent white," this due to the "boundless white racism" that existed across the Old South. We have already seen that the integrated South was far less racist than the segregated North, so it is obvious that this charge cannot be true. The South's army and navy, in fact, reflected the region's citizenship, which was made up of every race, creed, and nationality.

You are not supposed to know that uniformed, armed, and highly trained black Confederate soldiers, like this one, made up as much as 50 percent of the Rebel military force, proudly serving in a variety of capacities, from hostlers, nurses, and musicians, to spies, infantrymen, and sharpshooters.

Though—thanks to the vicious Yankee custom of burning down Southern courthouses—exact statistics are impossible to come by, Southern historians have determined that the following numbers are roughly accurate. In descending numerical order the Confederate army and navy was composed of about 1 million European-Americans, 300,000 to 1 million African-Americans, 70,000 Native-Americans, 60,000 Latin-Americans, 50,000 foreigners, 12,000 Jewish-Americans, and 10,000 Asian-Americans.

True Southerners, of all races, continue to be proud of our region's multiracial history, and of the many contributions made to Dixie by individuals of all colors, religions, and nations.[104]

FACT 76

THE CONFEDERATE STATES OF AMERICA HAD THE SUPPORT OF EUROPE

Mainstream history books would have us believe that the Southern Confederacy could not secure the support of Europe because she "practiced slavery." But again, this is false. The real reason Europe hesitated to give the South diplomatic recognition was because it feared offending and possibly provoking the U.S. into war, a frightening scenario that at one point almost became a reality.

Through Lincoln's secretary of state, William H. Seward, Lincoln privately threatened war on any nation that interfered with his invasion of the South, in particular England and France, where sympathy for the Confederacy was strongest. Lincoln's apprehension was

Though Lord Palmerston, British Prime Minister during America's "Civil War," fully supported the Confederacy, he backed away from lending her England's direct support due to Lincoln's threats of violence. France, like Britain, later specifically stated that "Southern slavery" had no effect on their decision.

warranted: England's and France's ruling classes were always highly interested in and supportive of the Confederate Cause, while the English population as a whole expressed "widespread sentiment" in favor of recognizing the Confederacy as a sovereign nation.

It was Lincoln's menacing warning, in place throughout the duration of the conflict, that prevented "neutral" Europe from publicly supporting "belligerent" Dixie, and which in turn prolonged the War, caused thousands of unnecessary deaths, and aided in the South's eventual downfall.[105]

FACT 77

THE CONFEDERATE BATTLE FLAG IS NOT A SYMBOL OF SLAVERY OR WHITE SUPREMACY

From the very beginning Dixie has been a multiracial, multiethnic, multicultural society, as is obvious from the region's military rolls, created during Lincoln's War. Under the beautiful Confederate Battle Flag (designed by my cousin Confederate General Pierre G. T. Beauregard), every known race donned Rebel gray or butternut and proudly and bravely defended Dixie against the Yankee invaders.

This proves to the world like nothing else can, that from the beginning the Confederacy fought, not to exploit and oppress the black race or any other race, but for the constitutional rights and personal freedom of all her people. Those who say anything different are either lying or are ignorant of genuine Southern history, plain and simple.

Some from the anti-Confederate Flag movement, like the racially intolerant Northern-based NAACP, know full well the true meaning of what we in Dixie call the "Southern Cross." Unfortunately, such groups (which even other blacks, like Reverend Jesse Lee Peterson, have labeled "hate groups") have a vested financial interest in fanning the flames of racism, for without the racial divisiveness created by their fake "race war," the world's race-baiters would go out of business.

Our most racist liberal president, Abraham Lincoln, thought along similar lines. He, along with the Radicals (that is, abolitionists) in his party, believed that by pitting whites and blacks against each other, the resulting tension, emotion, and fear would divide and weaken the South, allowing him to manipulate and overcome her people easier. Happily, Lincoln's attempt to poison Southern race relations failed, for the majority of whites and blacks saw through the ruse and remained loyal to one another both during and after his War.

The Confederate Battle Flag turns out to be anything but a symbol of slavery or white supremacy. Those who created it never intended it to have these meanings, and those who fought under it never thought of it in this way either. The descendants of those soldiers today have also never perceived it in this manner, as I myself can testify.

If anything it would be more accurate to call our flag a symbol of racial inclusiveness and multiculturalism, one founded on the Christian principles extolled by Jesus, whose main tenants were love and universal brotherhood. The Confederate Battle Flag itself was designed around the Christian crosses of Great Britain's flag (Saint George's Cross), Scotland's flag (Saint Andrew's Cross), and Ireland's flag (Saint Patrick's Cross).

Our beloved Battle Flag then, the winsome Southern Cross, is an emblem of not only small government, capitalism, personal liberty, and self-government, but also of American patriotism, strict constitutionalism, Christian love, and Southern heritage. Indeed, these are the very reasons that Conservative Confederate President Jefferson Davis described the Southern Confederacy as "the last best hope of liberty." As such, the Confederate Battle Flag is one that all Southerners, and all lovers of freedom, can revere unreservedly, as well as display with pride and honor whenever and wherever possible. Conservative Founder and Southern abolitionist Thomas Jefferson, the "Father of the Declaration of Independence," would heartily approve.[106]

FACT 78

THE MAJORITY OF NORTHERNERS
WERE ANTI-ABOLITIONISTS

Like Lincoln, the great majority of Northerners, including the Union armies, were anti-abolition and did not support the idea of nationwide emancipation. In fact, abolitionists made up only a tiny but loud minority in the North, as Lincoln himself was well aware.

Proof that the North was not truly an abolitionist area was that while it abolished slavery in its own backyard, the majority still did not want to end slavery in the South, for New England's textile mills, and the New York industrialists who owned them, were still making vast fortunes from Southern cotton, picked and ginned by millions of Southern servants. Thus, a full scale Northern effort began to keep Southern slavery alive, and even strengthen and enlarge it.

It was in this way that when the white North grew tired of dealing with blacks and slavery, she pushed the institution southward on a mostly unwilling populace, one that had been trying to officially abolish it since the early 1700s. For example, when New York slave owner John Bouiness freed one of his black servants in the North, at the same time he also had five other slaves sold in Virginia.

It has been estimated that at least 99 percent of Yankee businessmen were anti-abolitionists who supported the continuation of Southern slavery, for, as mentioned, the cotton that Southern slaves produced was one the North's largest financial assets. Among the most vociferous of this group were New York's "Wall Street Boys," which had bankrolled Lincoln's first (and later his second) presidential campaign using money they had made primarily from the Yankee slave trade. There was also the Boston elite, who made it known that they were quite willing to make huge concessions to the South in the interest of making money.

Around 1831 Rhode Islander Elizabeth Buffum Chace and her father Arnold Buffum, the first president of the New England Anti-Slavery Society, decided to travel across their region in order to enlist Yankee support for their emancipation plan. In her 1891 memoir Chace writes:

> I remember well, how eager we were, in our revived Anti-Slavery zeal, to present the cause of the slave to everybody we met [in New England]; not doubting that, when their attention was called to it, they would be ready, as we were, to demand his immediate emancipation. But, alas! their commercial relations, their political associations, and with many, their religious fellowship with the people of the South, so blinded the eyes, hardened the hearts and stifled the consciences of the North, that *we found very few people who were ready to give any countenance or support to the new AntiSlavery movement.*[107]

Prudence Crandall's "School for Colored Girls" being attacked and torched by local townspeople in Canterbury, Connecticut, in 1834. "Your nigger school shall never be allowed in Canterbury nor in any other town in this State!" the furious Yankee mob shouted. The building was later ripped from its foundation by a team of 100 oxen and burned. Crandall was only one of hundreds of Yankee abolitionists who were criticized, harassed, assaulted, and driven from the region for promoting racial equality. Her story highlights the utter disdain the majority of Northerners had for both blacks and abolition at the time.

Is it any wonder then that the 1860 Republican Party Platform contained paragraphs promising to leave the "peculiar institution" alone, while declaring that Republicans were only against the extension of slavery, not slavery itself? That in his First Inaugural Address, March 4, 1861, Lincoln pledged not to disturb slavery? Or that American slavery did not come to a final end until December 6, 1865 (eight months after Lincoln's death), with the passage of the Thirteenth Amendment?

Here we have more evidence, if more is needed, that the Civil War was not a contest over slavery. It was, in great part, a *Northern* contest over slavery money, a *Southern* contest over constitutional rights (that is, self-determination).[108]

FACT 79

LINCOLN'S EMANCIPATION PROCLAMATION DID NOT FREE A SINGLE SLAVE, & WAS NOT INTENDED TO

It is well-known to educated Southerners today that the Final Emancipation Proclamation, issued January 1, 1863, only "freed" slaves in the South, and even then, only in specific areas of the South. Lincoln's edict purposefully excluded Tennessee, for example (the entire state had been under Yankee control since the fall of Nashville, February 25, 1862), all of the Border States, and numerous Northern-occupied parishes in Louisiana and several counties in Virginia.

The Final Emancipation Proclamation, in fact, was issued only in areas of the South *not* under Union control; that is, it only "freed" *Southern* slaves who had sided with the Confederacy. It did not ban slavery anywhere in the North, where thousands of Yankees still practiced it, including Union officers like General Ulysses S. Grant and his family. As Lincoln states in the proclamation itself, the entire North, as well as those Southern places that were exempted, "are for the present left precisely as if this proclamation were not issued." He could not have made the meaning of this sentence more clear: *slavery was to be allowed to continue in the U.S. (that is, the North) and in any areas of the C.S. (that is, the South) controlled by the U.S. (that is, by the Union armies).*

The question Southerners have been asking Northerners for the past century and a half is why, if Lincoln was so interested in black equality, did he only abolish slavery in the South where he had no jurisdiction but not in the North where he had full control?

The answer is obvious to most Southerners today, just as it was to a majority of them in 1863: the Emancipation Proclamation was nothing more than a clever political illusion, for he did not free slaves where he legally could (in the North and in the Border States), yet he sought to free them (in the South) where he had no legal right to do so. If Northerners had asked themselves this same question at the time, they would have never created the myth of Lincoln the "Great Emancipator" to begin with!

In truth our sixteenth president did not issue the Emancipation Proclamation for the specific purpose of trying to establish black civil rights across the U.S. If that had indeed been his intention he would have also banned slavery in the North and in non-Union occupied areas of the South.

Being the penultimate politician, halfway through his war Lincoln decided that it would be politically expedient to shift the character of the conflict from "preserving the Union" to "abolishing slavery." Both were rank falsehoods, however, carefully calculated to procure Northern and abolitionist votes in the upcoming 1864 presidential election. Part of this devilish ruse was the issuance of the Final Emancipation Proclamation on January 1, 1863, which, revealingly, he publicly referred to not as a "civil rights measure," but as a "*war measure*"; not as a "civil rights emancipation," but as a "*military emancipation.*" Thus according to Lincoln himself, the edict did not have a single thing to do with black equality or even true abolition.

The Emancipation Proclamation was one of the greatest scams ever concocted in U.S. politics, by one of the most underhanded demagogues in American history. The truth about it is still being covered up to this day. But it is exposed here for all to see.

Yet, what a dastardly brilliant idea it was. For no one could argue against emancipation—not even the most pro-South Northerners or pro-North Southerners—if Lincoln could prove that freeing the slaves was vital to winning the War. Assuming that he would reap untold benefits from this shift in the character of the conflict from a political basis to a moral one, it did not matter whether or not any Southern slaves were actually freed to not. And thus legally none were.[109]

FACT 80

LINCOLN ONLY ISSUED THE EMANCIPATION PROCLAMATION FOR POLITICAL & MILITARY PURPOSES, NOT TO HELP AFRICAN-AMERICANS

D espite his cynical backroom conniving, President Lincoln did hope that his Emancipation Proclamation would yield results beyond merely garnering public support. But why did he wait nearly three years before issuing the document? If he was concerned about black civil rights, as pro-North advocates claim, why did he wait so long, only succumbing after years of pressure and harassment?[110]

The fact is that Lincoln issued the proclamation with five primary wishes in mind: 1) He hoped it would secure Europe's support. 2) He hoped it would instigate slave rebellions across the South. 3) He hoped to procure new troops to compensate for his drastically declining white soldiery. 4) He hoped to get new voters for the upcoming 1864 election. 5) He needed to free blacks before he could deport them.

Unfortunately for him, all five reasons were utter failures, for he was widely known among Southern blacks as a white racist who detested the abolitionist movement; who delayed abolition for as long as possible; was a leader in the American Colonization Society; forced slaves to complete the construction of the Capitol dome in Washington, D.C.; implemented extreme racist military policies; used profits from Northern slavery to fund his War; referred to blacks as "niggers"; said he was willing to allow slavery to continue in perpetuity if the Southern states would come back into the Union; engaged in a lifelong campaign to deport all American blacks; as a lawyer defended slave owners in court; backed the proslavery Corwin Amendment to the Constitution in 1861; and continually blocked black enlistment, black suffrage, and black citizenship. All of this is why Frederick Douglass said that Lincoln's attitude toward blacks lacked "the genuine spark of humanity."[111]

FACT 81

LINCOLN COMPARED FREED SLAVES TO WILD HOGS, DECLARING: "LET 'EM ROOT, PIG, OR PERISH!"

Lincoln had absolutely no formal plan for dealing with the millions of Southern slaves he intended to suddenly liberate in January 1863. If he truly cared about African-Americans, as we are asked to believe, this makes no sense whatsoever.

The reality is that he cared little for blacks, and he seldom tried to hide the fact. Once, when asked what was to become of emancipated blacks after they were "freed" by his Emancipation Proclamation, he likened them to wild hogs, and said: "Let 'em root, pig, or perish!"—and that is exactly what occurred, as our next entry shows.[112]

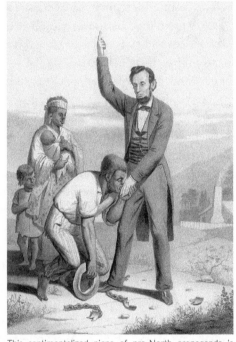

This sentimentalized piece of pro-North propaganda is meant to portray Lincoln's personal concern for black civil rights. No such scene ever took place, of course. In reality, Liberal Lincoln was a virulent racial bigot who barred blacks from the White House, used slaves to complete the dome on the U.S. Capitol building, and spent his entire adult life trying to deport African-Americans—whom he often referred to as "niggers" and an "inferior race." A two-faced rhetorician who would stop at nothing to get reelected, the Emancipation Proclamation turned out to be nothing but a nefarious ploy, just one part of the would-be dictator's plans to advance his tyrannical ambitions.

FACT 82

THE EMANCIPATION PROCLAMATION KILLED OFF 25 PERCENT OF ALL SOUTHERN BLACKS, MAKING IT AN EPIC NATIONAL DISASTER

After the issuance of the Emancipation Proclamation on January 1, 1863, only three things happened immediately: Union recruitment plummeted, Union desertion skyrocketed, and the quality of life for blacks sank to an all time low, remaining far beneath even slavery levels for the next 100 years.

After the War, for instance, black life span dropped 10 percent, diets and health deteriorated, disease and sickness rates went up 20 percent, the number of skilled blacks declined, and the gap between white and black wages widened, trends that did not even begin to reverse until the onset of World War II, 75 years later, in 1939. At least one out of four "freed" blacks died in a number of Southern communities.

Of life after January 1, 1863, Adeline Grey, a black South Carolina servant, wrote that when "liberation" came she could still vividly remember it, while slavery was but a dim memory. Why? Because "life was much more difficult and painful after emancipation than before."

The "pain" of emancipation was due, in great part, to the fact that Lincoln never pushed through any kind of organized, gradual, or compensated emancipation plan, as nearly every other Western nation had done when it abolished slavery. His proclamation, for example, contained no plans for freed black slaves, no provisions for housing, food, clothing, employment, or healthcare.

Freed slaves were merely "turned loose" to fend for themselves; literally cast out into the streets with no education, no jobs, no shelter, no job training, no grants or loans. The more unfortunate ended up on so-called "government plantations," malodorous squatter camps where poverty, sickness, hunger, thievery, and prostitution reigned.

And Lincoln's promise to freedmen of "forty acres and a mule" was little more than a carrot on the end of a stick, used to lure blacks into a false sense of governmental protection after emancipation. After all, his so-called "black land giveaways" were never meant to be permanent, and what little of these were dispersed went primarily to wealthy white Northerners.

Lincoln devotees enjoy sentimentalizing his Emancipation Proclamation. The truth is that the edict was illegal, unscrupulous, a failure, and one of America's most nightmarish debacles. Lincoln himself called it "the greatest folly of my life."

Under Lincoln's "root, pig, or perish" emancipation plan, blacks who as servants had lived quality lives equal to and often superior to many whites and free blacks, now found themselves living out in the open or in makeshift tents, begging for food and work. There was now less labor available to them under freedom than there had been under servitude, and thus the once booming Southern black economic system plunged.

Disease, homelessness, starvation, and beggary now became the lot of untold thousands of former black servants. Even many of those who managed to become sharecroppers eventually found themselves in a state of peonage (a debt that tied them to the land), living in crude filthy shacks, suffering from illiteracy, ill health, and malnutrition. All of this was a far cry from the excellent quality of life experienced by Southern blacks when they had lived under servitude. By 1867, just four years after the Emancipation Proclamation was issued, 1 million, or 25 percent, of all Southern blacks had perished from starvation, neglect, infanticide, corruption, and disease.

Due to how it was handled, the Emancipation Proclamation was truly a national disaster on an epic scale, as Lincoln himself admitted. It was "the greatest folly of my life," he later opined.[113]

FACT 83

NEARLY 100 PERCENT OF SOUTHERN BLACKS SUPPORTED THE CONFEDERACY

O f the South's 3.5 million black servants, the "vast majority," 95 percent (19 out of 20), remained in the South, all the while maintaining their loyalty to Dixie. Ignoring Lincoln's fake proclamation of freedom, they instead pledged their allegiance to their home states, to the South, and to their white families. Remaining at home they ran their owner's farm, grew food, produced provisions for the Confederate military, and protected their master's family and property while he was away on the battlefield. In 1910 Pastor Benjamin F. Riley noted that the Southern black servant

> sustained the armies of the Confederacy during the great Civil War; he was the guardian of the helpless women and children of the South while the husbands and sons were at the distant front doing battle . . .; against him was not a whisper of unfaithfulness or of disloyalty during all this trying and bloody period; when the land was invaded by the [Northern] armies . . . he remained faithful still, and often at great personal risk of life, secreted from the invader [his owner's] . . . horses and mules, and buried the treasures of the family that they might not fall into the hands of the enemies of the whites . . . . *he declined to accept freedom when it was offered by the invading army, preferring to remain loyal and steadfast to the charge committed to him by the absent master, all this and more the Negro slave did.* There was not a day during the trying period of the Civil War when he might not have disbanded the Southern armies. An outbreak on his part against the defenseless homes of the South would have occasioned the utter dissolution of the Southern armies, and turned the anxious faces of the veterans in gray toward their homes. But no Southern soldier ever dreamed of the possibility of a condition like this. So far as his home was concerned, it was not any apprehension of the unfaithfulness of the slaves which occasioned the slightest alarm.[114]

FACT 84

SLAVERY IS STILL BEING VIGOROUSLY PRACTICED AROUND THE WORLD, INCLUDING IN AFRICA & THE UNITED STATES

Contrary to popular opinion, slavery did not die out after Lincoln's phony Emancipation Proclamation in 1863. The institution continues to thrive and is universal in scope: according to Britain's Anti-Slavery Society, slavery is still found all over the world, even in the U.S., though it continues to flourish most consistently in Africa, the Middle East, the Far East, and in parts of South America.

Not only this, but studies reveal that the rate of slavery is actually increasing not decreasing, for *there are now more slaves in the world than at any other time in human history*: in 1933, 5 million slaves were estimated to exist around the globe. Yet, at the time of this

Black slaves in present day Africa.

writing, 2015, at least 30 million people are currently living under authentic slavery, while an additional 200 million people worldwide are suffering under one type of bondage or another. (Let us contrast these figures with the Old South, which never possessed more than 3.5 million servants, 86 percent of these, in 1860, which were American born.)

As for the U.S., according to a pre-2000 CIA study, 50,000 people (mostly women and children) were enslaved in the U.S. At the time of this survey, this number was expected to rise—and indeed it has. As of 2013 there were 60,000 slaves in the U.S. Both these slaves and their enslavers come in every race and color, more proof that slavery—whether modern, Victorian, Medieval, ancient, or prehistoric—is not, and never has been, based on skin color.[115]

NOTES

1. See Jones, TDMV, pp. 144, 200-201, 273.
2. See Seabrook, TAHSR, passim. See also, Pollard, LC, p. 178; Franklin, pp. 101, 111, 130, 149; Nicolay and Hay, ALCW, Vol. 1, p. 627.
3. See e.g., Seabrook, TQJD, pp. 30, 38, 76.
4. Seabrook, EYWTATCWIW, p. 13.
5. See Seabrook, TGYC, passim.
6. Seabrook, EYWTAASIW, pp. 45, 256-257.
7. Seabrook, EYWTAASIW, p. 127.
8. For more on the true history of prostitution, see my book *Aphrodite's Trade*.
9. Seabrook, EYWTAASIW, p. 60.
10. Seabrook, EYWTAASIW, pp. 62-64.
11. Seabrook, EYWTAASIW, p. 65.
12. Seabrook, EYWTAASIW, p. 279.
13. Seabrook, EYWTAASIW, pp. 87-88, 94-96.
14. Seabrook, EYWTAASIW, pp. 125-153.
15. Seabrook, EYWTAASIW, pp. 155-163.
16. Seabrook, EYWTAASIW, pp. 62-96, 155-163.
17. Seabrook, EYWTAASIW, pp. 65-66.
18. Seabrook, EYWTAASIW, pp. 108-114.
19. Seabrook, EYWTAASIW, pp. 108-110.
20. Emphasis added.
21. Seabrook, EYWTAASIW, p. 230. Emphasis added.
22. Work, p. 81.
23. Emphasis added.
24. Emphasis added.
25. Seabrook, EYWTAASIW, pp. 549-551, 570-571.
26. Seabrook, EYWTAASIW, pp. 48, 244.
27. Seabrook, EYWTAASIW, pp. 215-216.
28. Seabrook, EYWTAASIW, pp. 172, 216-219.
29. Seabrook, EYWTAASIW, pp. 220-222, 441.
30. Seabrook, EYWTAASIW, pp. 184, 197-198, 212, 657.
31. Seabrook, EYWTAASIW, p. 420.
32. Seabrook, EYWTAASIW, pp. 273, 426.
33. Seabrook, EYWTAASIW, pp. 270, 425-426.
34. Seabrook, EYWTAASIW, pp. 542-543. Emphasis added.
35. Seabrook, EYWTAASIW, p. 207. Emphasis added.
36. Seabrook, EYWTAASIW, pp. 182-183.
37. Seabrook, EYWTAASIW, pp. 459-460.
38. Lincoln called his "Emancipation Proclamation" exactly what it was: not a civil rights emancipation, but a "military emancipation." In other words, its true purpose was to "liberate" black servants, not so they could be free, but so the liberal Yankee president could use them in his armies. See e.g., Seabrook, L, p. 647.
39. Seabrook, EYWTAASIW, pp. 270, 329-330. Emphasis added.
40. Seabrook, EYWTAASIW, pp. 304-316, 321-322, 442, 668, 674, 796, 823.
41. Seabrook, EYWTAASIW, pp. 493-494. Emphasis added.
42. Seabrook, EYWTAASIW, pp. 583-584, 586.
43. Seabrook, EYWTAASIW, p. 347.
44. Seabrook, EYWTAASIW, pp. 647-648.
45. Seabrook, EYWTAASIW, pp. 647-648.

46. Emphasis added.
47. Emphasis added.
48. Seabrook, EYWTAASIW, pp. 649, 655-656.
49. Seabrook, EYWTAASIW, p. 653.
50. Seabrook, EYWTAASIW, pp. 654-655.
51. Seabrook, EYWTAASIW, pp. 106, 108, 251-252. Emphasis added.
52. Seabrook, EYWTAASIW, pp. 335-336.
53. Seabrook, EYWTAASIW, pp. 103-104. Emphasis added.
54. Seabrook, EYWTAASIW, pp. 799-802.
55. Seabrook, EYWTAASIW, pp. 524, 860-863. Emphasis added.
56. Seabrook, EYWTAASIW, p. 273.
57. Emphasis added.
58. Emphasis added.
59. Emphasis added.
60. For more on Stephens and his genuine attitude toward African-Americans, see Seabrook, TAHSR, passim; and Seabrook, TQAHS, passim.
61. Speeches, "Speech of Mr. Faulkner, of Virginia," p. 7.
62. Seabrook, EYWTAASIW, pp. 260-264.
63. Seabrook, EYWTAASIW, p. 280.
64. Seabrook, EYWTAASIW, pp. 96-108.
65. Seabrook, EYWTAASIW, pp. 174-175.
66. See Seabrook, AL, passim; Seabrook, TGI, passim; Seabrook, TUAL, passim; Seabrook, L, passim.
67. Seabrook, AL, p. 258.
68. Seabrook, EYWTAASIW, p. 220.
69. Seabrook, EYWTAASIW, p. 539. Emphasis added.
70. Seabrook, TAHSR, p. 11.
71. Seabrook, EYWTAASIW, p. 1014.
72. Seabrook, EYWTATCWIW, pp. 38-40; Seabrook, TUAL, p. 40.
73. Seabrook, EYWTAASIW, p. 522. Emphasis added.
74. Seabrook, EYWTAASIW, p. 524.
75. Seabrook, AL, pp. 47-48.
76. It is noteworthy that when the American Communist Party met at Chicago, Illinois, in 1939, they hung a gargantuan image of Lincoln in the center of the wall behind the speaker's platform. On either side of the stage were placed much smaller images of Lenin and Stalin. Another example of Lincoln's connection to the far Left comes from the same time period: in the late 1930s the American Communist Party formed (or assisted in forming) the "Abraham Lincoln Brigade," a battalion of volunteers who fought for Spain against the fascists during the Spanish Civil War. Nearly all of the Lincoln Brigade's soldiers were members of various communist and socialist organizations. For more on this topic, see Browder, passim; McCarty, passim; Benson and Kennedy, passim.
77. Seabrook, EYWTAASIW, pp. 507-508.
78. Seabrook, EYWTAASIW, p. 677.
79. Seabrook, EYWTAASIW, pp. 808, 814-815, 948.
80. Seabrook, AL, pp. 250, 355-356.
81. Emphasis added.
82. Seabrook, EYWTAASIW, pp. 784-785.
83. Seabrook, EYWTAASIW, pp. 242-243.
84. Seabrook, EYWTAASIW, pp. 599, 612.
85. Emphasis added.
86. Seabrook, EYWTAASIW, pp. 236-239, 745-754.
87. Work, p. 81.
88. Emphasis added.
89. Seabrook, EYWTAASIW, pp. 220, 571-572, 596, 622.
90. See Seabrook, C101, passim.
91. Seabrook, EYWTAASIW, p. 736.

92. Seabrook, EYWTAASIW, pp. 230-231, 541, 549, 571.

93. Seabrook, EYWTAASIW, p. 658. Emphasis added.

94. Seabrook, EYWTAASIW, pp. 244-249.

95. Liberal Lincoln was promoting anti-South Yankee propaganda here. The Conservative South never once demanded that "slavery ought to be extended." She only asked that individuals be given the choice as to whether or not they practiced slavery in the new Western Territories. After all, the institution was still legal under the Constitution at the time. As always, the South's main interest was the preservation of individual and states' rights, not the preservation of slavery.

96. Emphasis added.

97. Emphasis added.

98. Emphasis added.

99. Seabrook, EYWTAASIW, pp. 772-776.

100. Seabrook, EYWTAASIW, pp. 441-443.

101. Seabrook, C101, p. 98.

102. Seabrook, C101, p. 99.

103. Seabrook, C101, p. 100.

104. Seabrook, C101, p. 102.

105. Seabrook, C101, p. 103.

106. Seabrook, EYWTAASIW, pp. 395-397.

107. Emphasis added.

108. Seabrook, EYWTAASIW, pp. 240-242.

109. Seabrook, EYWTAASIW, pp. 609, 611, 686-688, 694.

110. Lincoln's procrastination toward issuing the Emancipation Proclamation earned him numerous unflattering titles from fellow Republicans, such as "the tortoise president" and "the slow coach at Washington." Seabrook, EYWTAASIW, p. 696.

111. Seabrook, EYWTAASIW, pp. 686-694, 732, 764.

112. Seabrook, EYWTAASIW, pp. 718-719.

113. Seabrook, EYWTAASIW, pp. 722-726, 810.

114. Seabrook, EYWTAASIW, pp. 689-690. Emphasis added.

115. Seabrook, EYWTAASIW, pp. 164-165.

BIBLIOGRAPHY

Bailey, Liberty Hyde (ed.). *Cyclopedia of Farm Animals*. New York, NY: Macmillan, 1922.

Benson, Al, Jr., and Walter Donald Kennedy. *Lincoln's Marxists*. Gretna, LA: Pelican Publishing, 2011.

Browder, Earl. *Lincoln and the Communists*. New York, NY: Workers Library Publishers, Inc., 1936.

Franklin, John Hope. *Reconstruction After the Civil War*. Chicago, IL: University of Chicago Press, 1961.

Jones, John William. *The Davis Memorial Volume; Or Our Dead President, Jefferson Davis and the World's Tribute to His Memory*. Richmond, VA: B. F. Johnson, 1889.

McCarty, Burke (ed.). *Little Sermons In Socialism by Abraham Lincoln*. Chicago, IL: The Chicago Daily Socialist, 1910.

Nicolay, John George, and John Hay (eds.). *Abraham Lincoln: Complete Works*. 12 vols. New York, NY: The Century Co., 1907.

Pollard, Edward Alfred. *The Lost Cause*. New York, NY: E. B. Treat and Co., 1867.

Seabrook, Lochlainn. *Abraham Lincoln: The Southern View*. 2007. Franklin, TN: Sea Raven Press, 2013 ed.

——. *A Rebel Born: A Defense of Nathan Bedford Forrest*. 2010. Franklin, TN: Sea Raven Press, 2011 ed.

——. *Everything You Were Taught About the Civil War is Wrong, Ask a Southerner!* 2010. Franklin, TN: Sea Raven Press, revised 2014 ed.

——. *The Quotable Jefferson Davis: Selections From the Writings and Speeches of the Confederacy's First President*. Franklin, TN: Sea Raven Press, 2011.

——. *Lincolnology: The Real Abraham Lincoln Revealed In His Own Words*. Franklin, TN: Sea Raven Press, 2011.

——. *The Unquotable Abraham Lincoln: The President's Quotes They Don't Want You To Know!* Franklin, TN: Sea Raven Press, 2011.

——. *The Great Impersonator: 99 Reasons to Dislike Abraham Lincoln*. Franklin, TN: Sea Raven Press, 2012.

——. *The Alexander H. Stephens Reader: Excerpts From the Works of a Confederate Founding Father*. Franklin, TN: Sea Raven Press, 2013.

——. *Everything You Were Taught About American Slavery War is Wrong, Ask a Southerner!* Franklin, TN: Sea Raven Press, 2015.

——. *Confederacy 101: Amazing Facts You Never Knew About America's Oldest Political Tradition*. Franklin, TN: Sea Raven Press, 2015.

——. *The Great Yankee Coverup: What the North Doesn't Want You to Know About Lincoln's War!* Franklin, TN: Sea Raven Press, 2015.

Speeches Made in the House of Representatives Upon the Kansas-Nebraska Bill. Washington, D.C.: Congressional Globe Office, 1854.

Work, Monroe N. (ed.). *Negro Year Book: An Annual Encyclopedia of the Negro, 1914-1915*. Tuskegee, AL: The Negro Year Book Publishing Co., 1914.

INDEX

MEET THE AUTHOR

OCHLAINN SEABROOK, winner of the prestigious Jefferson Davis Historical Gold Medal for his "masterpiece," *A Rebel Born: A Defense of Nathan Bedford Forrest*, is an unreconstructed Southern historian, award-winning author, Civil War scholar, and traditional Southern Agrarian of Scottish, English, Irish, Dutch, Welsh, German, and Italian extraction. An encyclopedist, lexicographer, musician, artist, graphic designer, genealogist, and photographer, as well as an award-winning poet, songwriter, and screenwriter, he has a 40 year background in historical nonfiction writing and is a member of the Sons of Confederate Veterans, the Civil War Trust, and the National Grange.

COPYRIGHT ©
SEA RAVEN PRESS

Lochlainn Seabrook, award-winning Civil War scholar & unreconstructed Southern historian.

Due to similarities in their writing styles, ideas, and literary works, Seabrook is often referred to as the "new Shelby Foote," the "Southern Joseph Campbell," and the "American Robert Graves" (his English cousin).

The grandson of an Appalachian coal-mining family, Seabrook is a seventh-generation Kentuckian, co-chair of the Jent/Gent Family Committee (Kentucky), founder and director of the Blakeney Family Tree Project, and a board member of the Friends of Colonel Benjamin E. Caudill. Seabrook's literary works have been endorsed by leading authorities, museum curators, award-winning historians, bestselling authors, celebrities, noted scientists, well respected educators, TV show hosts and producers, renowned military artists, esteemed Southern organizations, and distinguished academicians from around the world.

Seabrook has authored over 45 popular adult books on the American Civil War, American and international slavery, the U.S. Confederacy (1781), the Southern Confederacy (1861), religion, theology and thealogy, Jesus, the Bible, the Apocrypha, the Law of Attraction, alternative health, spirituality, ghost stories, the paranormal, ufology, social issues, and cross-cultural studies of the family and marriage. His Confederate biographies, pro-South studies, genealogical monographs, family histories, military encyclopedias, self-help guides, and etymological dictionaries have received wide acclaim.

Seabrook's eight children's books include a Southern guide to the Civil War, a biography of Nathan Bedford Forrest, a dictionary of religion and myth, a rewriting of the King Arthur legend (which reinstates the original pre-Christian motifs), two bedtime stories for preschoolers, a naturalist's guidebook to owls, a worldwide look at the family, and an examination of the Near-Death Experience.

Of blue-blooded Southern stock through his Kentucky, Tennessee, Virginia, West Virginia, and North Carolina ancestors, he is a direct descendant of European royalty via his 6th great-grandfather, the Earl of Oxford, after which London's famous Harley Street is named. Among his celebrated male Celtic ancestors is Robert the Bruce, King of Scotland, Seabrook's 22nd great-grandfather. The 21st great-grandson of Edward I "Longshanks" Plantagenet), King of England, Seabrook is a thirteenth-generation Southerner through his descent from the colonists of Jamestown, Virginia (1607).

The 2nd, 3rd, and 4th great-grandson of dozens of Confederate soldiers, one of his closest connections to Lincoln's War is through his 3rd great-grandfather, Elias Jent, Sr., who fought for the Confederacy in the Thirteenth Cavalry Kentucky under Seabrook's 2nd cousin, Colonel Benjamin E. Caudill. The Thirteenth, also known as "Caudill's Army," fought in numerous conflicts, including the Battles of Saltville, Gladsville, Mill Cliff, Poor Fork, Whitesburg, and Leatherwood.

Seabrook is a descendant of the families of Alexander H. Stephens, John Singleton Mosby, William Giles Harding, and Edmund Winchester Rucker, and is related to the following Confederates and other 19th-Century luminaries: Robert E. Lee, Stephen Dill Lee, Stonewall Jackson, Nathan Bedford Forrest, James Longstreet, John Hunt Morgan, Jeb Stuart, Pierre G. T. Beauregard (approved the Confederate Battle Flag design), George W. Gordon, John Bell Hood, Alexander Peter Stewart, Arthur M. Manigault, Joseph Manigault, Charles Scott Venable, Thornton A. Washington, John A. Washington, Abraham Buford, Edmund W. Pettus, Theodrick "Tod" Carter, John B. Womack, John H. Winder, Gideon J. Pillow, States Rights Gist, Henry R. Jackson, John Lawton Seabrook, John C. Breckinridge, Leonidas Polk, Zachary Taylor, Sarah Knox Taylor (first wife of Jefferson Davis), Richard Taylor, Davy Crockett, Daniel Boone, Meriwether Lewis (of the Lewis and Clark Expedition) Andrew Jackson, James K. Polk, Abram Poindexter Maury (founder of Franklin, TN), Zebulon Vance, Thomas Jefferson, Edmund Jennings Randolph, George Wythe Randolph (grandson of Jefferson), Felix K. Zollicoffer, Fitzhugh Lee, Nathaniel F. Cheairs, Jesse James, Frank James, Robert Brank Vance, Charles Sidney Winder, John W. McGavock, Caroline E. (Winder) McGavock, David Harding McGavock, Lysander McGavock, James Randal McGavock, Randal William McGavock, Francis McGavock, Emily McGavock, William Henry F. Lee, Lucius E. Polk, Minor Meriwether (husband of noted pro-South author Elizabeth Avery Meriwether), Ellen Bourne Tynes (wife of Forrest's chief of artillery, Captain John W. Morton), South Carolina Senators Preston Smith Brooks and Andrew Pickens Butler, and famed South Carolina diarist Mary Chesnut.

Seabrook's modern day cousins include: Patrick J. Buchanan (conservative author), Cindy Crawford (model), Shelby Lee Adams (Letcher Co., Kentucky, photographer), Bertram Thomas Combs (Kentucky's 50th governor), Edith Bolling (wife of President Woodrow Wilson), and actors Robert Duvall, Reese Witherspoon, Lee Marvin, Rebecca Gayheart, Andy Griffith, and Tom Cruise.

Seabrook's screenplay, *A Rebel Born*, based on his book of the same name, has been signed with acclaimed filmmaker Christopher Forbes (of Forbes Film). It is now in pre-production, and is set for release in 2016 as a full-length feature film. This will be the first movie ever made of Nathan Bedford Forrest's life story, and as a historically accurate project written from the Southern perspective, is destined to be one of the most talked about Civil War films of all time.

Born with music in his blood, Seabrook is an award-winning, multi-genre, BMI-Nashville songwriter and lyricist who has composed some 3,000 songs (250 albums), and whose original music has been heard in film (*A Rebel Born, Cowgirls 'n Angels, Confederate Cavalry, Billy the Kid: Showdown in Lincoln County, Vengeance Without Mercy, Last Step, County Line, The Mark*) and on TV and radio worldwide. A musician, producer, multi-instrumentalist, and renown performer—whose keyboard work has been variously compared to pianists from Hargus Robbins and Vince Guaraldi to Elton John and Leonard Bernstein—Seabrook has opened for groups such as the Earl Scruggs Review, Ted Nugent, and Bob Seger, and has performed privately for such public figures as President Ronald Reagan, Burt Reynolds, Loni Anderson, and Senator Edward W. Brooke. Seabrook's cousins in the music business include: Johnny Cash, Elvis Presley, Billy Ray and Miley Cyrus, Patty Loveless, Tim McGraw, Lee Ann Womack, Dolly Parton, Pat Boone, Naomi, Wynonna, and Ashley Judd, Ricky Skaggs, the Sunshine Sisters, Martha Carson, and Chet Atkins.

Seabrook, a libertarian, lives with his wife and family in historic Middle Tennessee, the heart of Forrest country and the Confederacy, where his conservative Southern ancestors fought valiantly against Liberal Lincoln and the progressive North in defense of Jeffersonianism, constitutional government, and personal liberty.

LochlainnSeabrook.com

If you enjoyed this book you will be interested in Mr. Seabrook's other popular related titles:

☛ EVERYTHING YOU WERE TAUGHT ABOUT AMERICAN SLAVERY IS WRONG, ASK A SOUTHERNER!
☛ EVERYTHING YOU WERE TAUGHT ABOUT THE CIVIL WAR IS WRONG, ASK A SOUTHERNER!
☛ CONFEDERACY 101: AMAZING FACTS YOU NEVER KNEW ABOUT AMERICA'S OLDEST POLITICAL TRADITION
☛ THE CONSTITUTION OF THE CONFEDERATE STATES OF AMERICA EXPLAINED

Available from Sea Raven Press and wherever fine books are sold

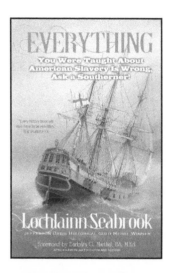

SeaRavenPress.com